The last thing this world needs is just another self-improvement book. That's why I'm so excited about *When You, Then God*. Rusty George writes with an urgency to awaken all who are simply coasting through life. If you just want to live an ordinary life, with God as a side dish, then don't pick up this book. In *When You, Then God*, you will be reminded anew of the power and purpose of our great God. It is refreshingly inspirational and challenging at the same time.

PETE WILSON
Senior pastor of Cross Point Church, Nashville, Tennessee

Rusty George is a tremendous leader and a powerful voice for what it means to walk in faith in today's complicated world. In this book, Rusty's transparency will move you to experience more of God and his incredible hope in your life.

JUD WILHITE
Senior pastor of Central Christian Church, Las Vegas, and author of *Pursued*

This book is a gift to those who find their spiritual life exhausting. For twenty years, I spun plates and juggled oranges like a crazy woman, trying to make God happy. It was only when everything fell that I discovered the profound truth that Rusty outlines in this powerful book: God simply loves being with you—as you are, right now. Together, you might even change the world.

SHEILA WALSH
Author of *Five Minutes with Jesus*

One of the most overlooked principles in Scripture is the simple fact that how we respond to God actually matters. The Bible is filled with if/then statements that somehow get turned into blanket promises and empty threats. In *When You, Then God*, Rusty George unpacks many of the most important, most forgotten, and most misunderstood conditional statements in Scripture.

LARRY OSBORNE
Author, and pastor of North Coast Church, Vista, California

Rusty George is the real deal, a humble and sincere follower of Jesus. In this book, he vulnerably shares some of his greatest discoveries—not about serving God, but about knowing God and embracing God's love deeply, personally, and transformationally. It was life changing for Rusty, and it will be for you, too.

GENE APPEL
Senior pastor of Eastside Christian Church, Anaheim, California

Rusty is fluent in the language of freedom, and he offers a map to every reader seeking a grace-filled journey toward hope. The pages of this book will lead you into the parts of your head and heart that need to be explored if you are to experience the life that Jesus died to give you. By the end of the book, you'll find the rest you've been looking for.

JON WEECE
Author of *Me Too*

Sensible. Encouraging. And, best of all, biblical. Rusty has written an easy-to-read, very practical book that I believe will be helpful to the body of Christ. You'll be challenged and set free to walk closer to your Savior.

RON EDMONDSON
Senior pastor of Immanuel Baptist Church, Lexington, Kentucky

WHEN YOU, THEN GOD

when you, then God

7 things God is waiting to do in your life

RUSTY GEORGE

WITH MICHAEL DEFAZIO

TYNDALE®
MOMENTUM

AN IMPRINT OF
TYNDALE HOUSE PUBLISHERS, INC.

Visit Tyndale online at www.tyndale.com.

Visit Tyndale Momentum online at www.tyndalemomentum.com.

Tyndale Momentum and the Tyndale Momentum logo are registered trademarks of Tyndale House Publishers, Inc. Tyndale Momentum is an imprint of Tyndale House Publishers, Inc.

When You, Then God: Seven Things God Is Waiting to Do in Your Life

Designed by Dean H. Renninger

Published in association with the literary agent Don Gates of The Gates Group, www.the-gates-group.com.

The stories in this book are about real people and real events, but some names have been changed for the privacy of the individuals involved.

Library of Congress Cataloging-in-Publication Data
Names: George, Rusty, date, author.
Title: When you, then God : seven things God is waiting to do in your life /
  Rusty George, with Michael DeFazio.
Description: Carol Stream, IL : Tyndale House Publishers, Inc., 2016. |
  Includes bibliographical references.
Identifiers: LCCN 2015040871 | ISBN 9781496406040 (sc)
Subjects: LCSH: God (Christianity)—Promises. | Obedience—Biblical teaching.
Classification: LCC BT180.P7 G48 2016 | DDC 248.4—dc23 LC record available at http://lccn
  .loc.gov/2015040871

Printed in the United States of America

22	21	20	19	18	17	16
7	6	5	4	3	2	1

For Lorrie, Lindsey, and Sidney
When you . . . came into my life,
then God . . . was doubly good to me.

contents

foreword

by Kyle Idleman

This may sound strange, but I've always enjoyed the experience of going to a car lot and negotiating for a used car. For most people, haggling with a used-car salesman ranks right up there with going to the dentist for a root canal. But I'm competitive by nature, and getting the best possible price feels like a win to me. I realize that most people aren't wired that way and that we're all a little afraid of being taken advantage of or feeling as if we could've gotten more for our money.

Whether or not you enjoy the negotiation process, it's hard to avoid it in our consumer-based culture. In fact, "everything is negotiable" is one of the great mantras of the Western world.

Negotiations tend to be "when/then" transactions: *When* I give you *this . . . then* you will give me *that*. We negotiate these When/Then agreements not only in our economic transactions but also in our relationships. It may be on a subconscious level, but we're afraid of being shortchanged. So we are careful to look out for ourselves, making sure we aren't giving any more than we have to and that we are getting everything we deserve in return.

I am convinced that, perhaps without meaning to, we often turn our relationship with God into a similar negotiation. Following Jesus becomes a When/Then agreement where we are careful not to give up more than we are required to and that we get what's coming to us.

What I love about *When You, Then God* is that it helps us understand that the When/Then teachings in Scripture are not transactions to be negotiated but blessings that have been promised by God. God is not a negotiator who is holding out on us until he gets what he wants, where we lose and he wins.

So as you begin this book, can I challenge you to lower your defenses? God isn't trying to take advantage of you. You don't need to wonder whether he's holding out on you or whether you can get a better deal down the road. God already showed all his cards and gave up his negotiating position when he gave his only Son.

In *When You, Then God*, Rusty George holds nothing back. Read this book and learn that God is on your side. He's a giver, and he wants you to experience abundant life in him.

preface:
NOT THAT KIND OF BOOK

I'll be honest: I don't need another book telling me to take a leap and change the world. I don't know about you, but the shelves in my office are well stocked with books imploring me to take a risk, walk across the room, lend a hand, give a dollar, or just make a decision and change the world. On top of that, the Kindle app on my iPad is loaded with even more books pleading with me to be the difference, make a stand, burn the ships, and refuse to lose. I get the message.

Though all those books make good points, they also make me feel pretty guilty. In fact, just sitting here writing this preface while drinking a hot cup of coffee in the comfort of my own home—complete with running water, indoor plumbing, and a refrigerator full of food—I feel guilty enough. In the time I've taken to write this paragraph, countless needs—*real* needs—have gone unmet around the world. And yet here I sit, sipping Sumatran coffee, when I could be *in* Sumatra changing the world.

If you're like me, your inbox is flooded with news of global epidemics that need your awareness. Every time you scroll through your social media, you see more videos, more Kickstarter campaigns, and more urgent appeals to help save everything from the whales to the rain forest to whales in the rain forest. (That's the worst kind.)

We know the world needs to change. And we've all heard the stories of those who have changed it: the elderly woman who saved all her pennies for eighty years and helped to fund a library for kids when she died; or the little boy who used the profits from a lemonade stand to furnish microloans for farmers in Kenya. These are the stories that make the news and create great opening vignettes for books about changing the world.

But that's not even the half of it. I also don't need another book about changing my own personal world.

Walk through any bookstore and you'll find entire sections devoted to self-improvement. Everything from how to lose weight to how to make a million dollars to how to be a perfect parent. We Christians are often quick to judge these books as worldly or New Age, but I have plenty of Christian titles on my shelves that promise the same things—except that they assign the work to God. God can cause the pounds to melt away, the millions to come my way, and my kids to never stray. All I need to do is learn a special prayer to pray, a certain way to fast, or a hidden discipline only recently discovered or rediscovered. On top of that are apps to download, verses to memorize, and five steps to success. If I work the plan, God is obligated to give me what I want. I just need to learn the secret of saying "pretty please."

Don't get me wrong. I'm not saying that I don't need to change or that changing the world is a bad idea. But without one key component, all those appeals and strategies fall on deaf ears. I've discovered that what I *really* need is to know beyond a shadow of a doubt—to *feel* and *experience* in the depths of my being—the truth that God loves me unconditionally, just as I am, without one plea. When the truth of God's love seeps into my marrow, then I am set free to love other people, serve them with a full heart, and walk in harmonious partnership with my Creator.

When that happens, no one has to tell me to leap . . . because I'm already in the arms of the Savior.

ready to

J

U

M

P

?

When my daughters were young and we'd go to the pool, we would often play that game where Dad stands about four feet from the side, in chest-deep water, and tries to convince the kids to jump to him. From the father's perspective, there is zero risk to this game, but you wouldn't know it by watching the kids quivering and shivering on the deck.

Like most little kids, my girls would inch forward toward the edge, filled with equal parts excitement and anxiety, and we'd start the familiar exchange.

"Jump," I would say.

"Daddy? Will you catch me?"

"Yes! Just jump."

"Are you sure you'll catch me?"

"Yes! Trust me! Just jump."

"Are you *sure* you'll catch me?"

"Yes. When you jump, then I'll catch you. But I can't prove that I'll catch you until you jump!"

This banter would go on for some time while I waited patiently for one girl or the other to crank up enough courage to fling herself from the side of the pool. All the while, I was moving closer and closer, until finally they could simply fall into my arms and let me ease them into the water.

As grown-ups who can stand up in four feet of water and who know how to swim, we may laugh at the little kids cowering on the pool deck. But let's be honest: *Jumping can be scary business.* Especially when we can't see exactly where we're going to land, or when we're not entirely certain that Daddy is going to catch us. Let's talk about some of the things we fear when it comes to trusting God.

Maybe we're afraid because, deep down, we're convinced that God is angry with us—that he wants to punish us. We know we're not perfect; we know we don't quite measure up to God's perfect standard, and maybe—just maybe—he wants to teach us a lesson by letting us hit the water and go under. If I think God is angry with me, I'm probably going to stay on the side of the pool. Wouldn't you?

Deep down, we're convinced that God is angry with us—that he wants to punish us.

Or maybe we're not afraid of God's anger as much as we're fearful of what we might have to give up if we fully surrender our lives to him. Do I have to quit my job and become a pastor or a missionary? Do I have to downsize my house or move to the inner city? Do I have to get rid of my Mercedes (or at least put a fish decal on the back)? What about my dreams, my aspirations, and my desire to succeed in life? Doesn't God allow for those things?

Many of our fears surround our occupations. We fear losing some relational advantages at the office if people find out we've become Jesus followers. Or we might be afraid that, by choosing a life of loving God and loving others, we'll lose our killer instinct at work and endanger our livelihood. Perhaps we fear that a transformation of our ethics and values will adversely affect our business.

Sometimes our fears are centered on our reputation. We could lose social status, jeopardize lifelong friendships, or risk rejection by certain clubs or social groups. We might even be perceived as weak, unintelligent, and out of touch or as bigoted, judgmental, and mean.

Maybe our fears are based simply on our desire for pleasure and comfort. If we decide to go all-in on following Jesus, will we have to give up our new car, downsize our home, or change our vacation plans? What will God call us to do if we decide to take that leap? Whatever it is, we're afraid that he'll somehow let us down and that we'll regret our decision to jump.

Or maybe at the heart of it, our fear is exactly the same as the one we have when we're perched on the side of the pool: We're afraid that Daddy isn't going to catch us. Maybe we've already jumped once or twice and it didn't turn out so well—at least according to our expectations. Maybe we're thinking that God hasn't come through for us or that life would be easier if we could go back to the way things used to be. Maybe things would be better if we could ease up on the Jesus stuff and take back control of our lives. That's fear talking. And it's perfectly natural.

But the Bible says that perfect love drives out fear.[1] So how do we get past it? Let's go back to the pool and see what helped my daughters to overcome their fear and trust my ability—and my commitment—to catch them when they jumped.

First of all, when I seemed *really* far away (maybe four

feet, in reality), they were far less inclined to jump. So I started gradually moving toward them. In a sense, this is the same approach God has taken with fearful humanity down through the ages.

Throughout the Bible, we're able to see how, after the Fall, God began to draw steadily closer to humanity again. At first, he was a voice from beyond the clouds. Then he became visible as a pillar of fire and a massive cloud leading the way through the wilderness. Next, he came into the midst of the people in the Tabernacle, and later in the Temple once the Israelites were permanently established in Jerusalem. When they still didn't quite get it, he came so close that he was human—Jesus! But then he said, "I'll get even closer. I'll move right into your life . . . and I'll unleash the transformative power of my Spirit to change you from the inside out." Imagine that: the very Spirit of God taking up residence inside us.

After the Fall, God began to draw steadily closer to humanity again.

With every step closer, God proved his love for us. He proved his commitment to us. He is a faithful God who deserves our trust. As we stand on the edge of the pool with our shaky faith, our heavenly Father moves close enough for us to fall into his arms. But we still have to step off the edge. As we contemplate the roiling surface of the water and ask, "Can I trust you?" God stands ever so close and says, "*When* you jump, *then* I'll catch you. But I can't prove it until you jump."

Okay, but how do we know for sure that we can trust God to keep us from drowning? In a word, it comes down to *love*. When my daughters stood shivering on the side of the pool, trying to exercise their faith in me, they already knew that I loved them with all my heart—I'm their daddy. They already knew I would do anything to protect them. They already knew I wouldn't let them sink to the bottom of the pool. Well . . . they were pretty sure about that last one.

It works the same way with God. If we know that he loves us, it's a whole lot easier to trust him with our lives. But what if we don't know? What if our faith is more theoretical than actual—more abstract belief than true knowledge? Trusting someone with our lives, our hopes, and our dreams can seem counterintuitive. It's hard enough to trust the people we live with every day, let alone a God we've never seen. We all know what it's like to pray big prayers yet cross our fingers. And when it comes to trusting that God really loves us with no strings attached, it feels like we're taking a big gamble. I once heard a preacher say, "God has revealed himself enough to inspire trust but hidden himself enough to require faith."[2] As much as I take comfort in that, he could help the trust part with a little more *revealing*.

> If we know that God loves us, it's a whole lot easier to trust him with our lives.

When someone tells us to trust God, it's easy to assume that it's all our responsibility. We picture God as some kind of talent scout, looking for prospective stars—as if he's watching from afar, waiting to see whether we're worth his time. In my case, viewing God this way caused me to doubt that he was trustworthy.

Love Deficit

I'll never forget the day I realized that I didn't believe God really loved me. And that I didn't love him either.

Even though by that point I had been a Christian for more than twenty-five years and a pastor for more than ten, most of my life had been built on rules and regulations—performance-based measures—and it had finally caught up with me.

My family was about a year into a new ministry in California; and with the logistics of moving across the country, the challenge of leading a young church, and the excitement of living on the West Coast, I hadn't paid much attention to the condition of my soul. Not long after I started the new job, I knew I was in trouble. I felt dead inside. I was doing all the right things as far as I knew—reading my Bible, praying, working hard at teaching and leading—but it felt like I was swimming in peanut butter.

In hindsight, I knew I had been feeling this way for a long time—I just hadn't wanted to admit it. Though I *talked* about God as a loving Father, I honestly had a hard time accepting his love for myself. No matter what I did, I felt there was so much more I could and should be doing.

Some years earlier, I had spent a day at a monastery in the hills of Kentucky, several hours from our home at the time. I'd heard stories about the monks and their devotion to God, and I thought, *Why not drive out there and spend some time with the monks?* Maybe they'd know something that would help me. I owned a pair of Birkenstocks, and maybe that was all it would take: walking the hillsides for a few hours in some hip sandals and soaking in the atmosphere. Sure enough, after a time of reading and praying and walking, I felt closer to God. But as I drove home, the familiar pressure returned, and any sense I'd had of God's pleasure in me vanished. And I was even still wearing my Birkenstocks!

In more recent years, I remembered some great days of ministry when I thought our weekend service really hit it out of the park. We served people, we led them to Jesus, and we exalted his name. In the afterglow, I sensed that my heavenly Father was smiling at me. But when Monday morning dawned, I was back to square one again. How could I duplicate or build upon what had just happened? If I'm honest, the thought that kept running through my head was this: *What would I do next to impress God?* As it had been throughout my life, my mind-set was one of trying to *change the world for God.* Unfortunately, but not surprisingly, I felt as if it were all up to me.

On a hot, windy day in the middle of March, I hopped on a plane at the Burbank airport and flew to Las Vegas to spend the day with an old friend and fellow pastor. Shane was pastoring a growing church that had strong similarities to my own. I wish I could tell you that I went to see him because I thought he could help me in my relationship with

God, but truthfully, I went to see whether he could help me get better at my job. Deep down, I still believed that if I did my job better and tried to be a better person, then God would be happy with me. I had no idea how much this mind-set affected every decision I made.

As I made my way through the Las Vegas airport, I saw Shane waiting for me. He gave me a huge hug, told me he was glad to see me, and suggested we get some lunch. It had been five years since I had seen him, and his hair was grayer and thinner than I remembered. But I guess mine was, too. Shane and I had grown up in the same church in Wichita, and we had taken very similar paths into ministry. We'd attended the same Bible college in order to become pastors—though he was four years ahead of me—and now we both were serving at churches in places way out of our comfort zones.

Because Shane's church was about a year ahead of mine in seemingly every aspect, I thought, *Who better to teach me how to lead a growing church than a close friend who knows where I'm coming from?* I went expecting to get a tour of his new building and pick up a few good tips about how to succeed in church growth and strategic planning. Surely Shane could help me become more successful so that I'd *feel* more successful.

At a quaint Italian restaurant in the heart of Las Vegas—who knew that a restaurant on the Strip could actually be quaint?—we reminisced about our youth-group days in Wichita, shared stories of friends past and present, and caught up with news of each other's family. Even though it had been years since I'd seen Shane, we picked up where we had left off. Shane had always been like a big brother to me, a mentor in life and ministry; and the years and distance had not diminished his ability to influence my life. As the meal concluded, we sat back with cups of hot coffee and began to get into church matters. It wasn't long before Shane began to unpack some church-growth secrets his church had found successful. We talked about sermon prep, calendar planning, and strategic processes.

After lunch, I was anxious to see their new building. At Real Life Church, we were in the process of planning our first construction project, and I thought I'd get some great ideas. It never hurts to ask the question, *What would you do differently?*

We arrived at the beautiful campus of Shane's church, which has a panoramic view of the desert and the Las Vegas skyline off in the distance. The church is strategically located in the suburbs where much of Vegas's workforce lives and raises kids. We walked the campus, and he showed me the offices, which were well laid out with room to grow. He showed me through the children's-ministry space, perfectly situated near the auditorium and with outdoor play areas for each room. And then we entered the auditorium, a fantastic space that not only held hundreds of people every Sunday but also could be reconfigured for events during the week. I officially had church building envy.

I was ready to pepper Shane with more questions, but I was not prepared for what happened next. He led me toward the back of the auditorium and into a decision room designed for people who want to pray or talk with someone after a service. When Shane suggested that we sit and talk some more, I grabbed a seat on one of the comfortable couches, and he sat down across from me in an oversize armchair. Before I could say another word, he started asking me some questions that, quite honestly, made me a bit uncomfortable.

"How's your relationship with God?" he asked.

"Good, I guess," I replied. That might have been an exaggeration.

"Define *good*."

"Well, you know . . . I miss my quiet time once in a while, but I'm studying for messages."

We laughed at my answer. We both knew the issue was bigger than that.

Shane continued his inquiry. "What are you afraid of?"

Part of me wanted to check my watch to see whether it was time to leave for the airport yet. But part of me was glad that someone had finally asked me the question.

What *was* I afraid of? Shane was digging right into my fear of failure, my insecurities about leading a church, and the overwhelming inadequacies I faced every day.

After a few moments of uncomfortable silence, during which I thought of every possible way to change the subject and move to a more comfortable topic of conversation, I decided to answer Shane's penetrating question.

Even though I'd been at the church in California for a little more than a year, I knew I was in way over my head. I had a church staff who looked to me for leadership and vision; I had a congregation who looked to me for spiritual depth and understanding; and I had a young family at home who looked to me for security and provision every single day. This was way more than I had learned about in Bible college, and I was feeling overwhelmed. I had trouble sleeping. I spent many nights wondering whether God was just quiet or whether I'd made him mad and chased him away. I still believed that God had led me to California to pastor this church, but I was beginning to wonder whether he had come with me. The more I tried to do all the right things, the more pressure I felt and the more it seemed I wasn't measuring up. Nothing seemed to help.

Shane was sympathetic. He leaned back in his seat, kicked up his feet onto the coffee table between us, and began to unpack a short and simple passage of Scripture for me. I had heard it before, but never quite this way.

"We love because he first loved us," Shane said, quoting 1 John 4:19.[3] "But if we love God because he first loved us . . . and we don't believe that he loves us . . . then we can't love him back, can we?"

That's when it hit me: *I didn't believe that God loved me.* I knew he put up with me and wanted to use me to advance his Kingdom. And I believed that he had gifted me and called me to teach and lead his church. But deep down in my soul, I wasn't convinced that he *loved* me. In fact, I was pretty sure he didn't like me much at all. He was definitely not impressed with anything I'd done—because I had not done enough to change the world for him. So why would I ever expect him to do anything to change *my* world?

If I couldn't accept that God loved me, how could I ever love him in return? I feared him; I wanted to impress him and make him happy; I wanted others to love him—but I didn't love him myself. And now I knew that I *couldn't*.

> If I couldn't accept that God loved me, how could I ever love him in return?

I don't remember anything else from the rest of the conversation—or the rest of the trip, for that matter. Shane took me back to the airport, and I flew home with a lot to process. What Shane had said explained so much of the frustration I had felt off and on for years. Because I didn't really believe that God loved me, it was difficult for me to trust him. And because I didn't trust him, I was left to my own devices, trapped in a performance-based religious faith.

Maybe that's why something inside me cringed whenever I told someone about the depths of God's love. I believed he loved other people, but that belief didn't extend to *me*—not if I was honest with myself. I told people that God could forgive them. But I wasn't entirely certain it applied to me. Maybe that's why, when I stood on the stage at Real Life Church and told the thousands of people in the congregation about God's passionate pursuit of them, I felt as if I should cross my fingers behind my back.

For the ten years of ministry before that point, I had been

preaching about God's love. But I hadn't really accepted it for myself.

If you had pressed me, I would have said that I believed I was going to heaven, but I wasn't sure how much hell I'd have to go through before I got there. After all, trying to impress God seemed an impossible feat in my mind.

Maybe you've felt the same way at some point in your life. Maybe you're feeling that way right now.

Our inability to believe that God loves us is often rooted in two flawed approaches to faith that I call the Thou Shalts and the Never Minds. Before I tell you about my own journey to discovering the truth about God's love for me, let's take a closer look at the devastating results of trying to operate our relationship with God through either of these two faulty systems.

chapter two:

THOU
SHALTS
AND
NEVER
MINDS

If you hang around long enough with a group of people, you begin to notice that they have their own language. Whether it's a clique of junior high girls, a college football team, or an office full of real-estate agents, each group has a common vocabulary among its members. This is normal, and it's not a problem—unless an outsider is expected to understand it. Then it gets difficult.

Whenever I fly, I'm always amazed at how the flight attendants use language that nobody else would use and that nobody else on the plane understands. For instance, I don't think I've ever said to my wife, "This weekend, there are several things we need to stow in the attic." I've never told my kids to make sure they use the lavatory before bed. And I have no idea what a cross-check is, or how the flight crew knows when it's finished so we can exit the plane. (On the other hand, I *do* know how to put on a seat belt, and yet they insist on teaching me on every flight.)

I often feel the same way around teachers. Spend an afternoon with a group of elementary school educators and you will hear words like *rubric*, *standardized testing*, *IEPs*, and many other acronyms that I'm pretty sure they invented just to make me feel stupid.

But the church is perhaps the most common place for specialized language. Think about some of the words and phrases we use that are never used anywhere else. For instance, some church buildings have a narthex. Good luck finding that. Not only do we use words like *fellowship*, but we also often build a room in our churches called the "fellowship hall." But most of us have never heard a neighbor say, "Hey, I'm getting the pay-per-view fight on Saturday night. Why don't you come over for some sweet fellowship?"

Occasionally you'll hear a "hallelujah" or "praise the Lord" at a basketball game, but those terms are mainly used in church. Moreover, no one knows what "traveling mercies" are, and I'm pretty sure that "bless your heart" just means "you're an idiot."

There's another phrase often used in church that I've had some trouble with. I'm referring to "the unconditional love of God." That always sounds too good to be true, and it's been my experience that most things that sound too good to be true probably are.

But let's take a closer look.

Perhaps the most vivid example of God's unconditional love is found in the parable of the Prodigal Son in Luke 15. The rebellious younger son in this story does far more than get a tattoo without permission and stay out past curfew. He demands to receive his inheritance on the spot and heads to Vegas to sow his wild oats. It isn't long before he's out of money, out of food, and out of luck. After hitting rock bottom, he begins the long journey back home, rehearsing his apology along the way.

> The most vivid example of God's unconditional love is found in the parable of the Prodigal Son.

While the prodigal is still a long way from the house, his

father sees him out on the road and comes running to meet him. It turns out that he's been waiting and watching for his son's return. Dad asks no questions, refuses any explanation, and won't even let the boy finish his apology. Instead, he throws a party to celebrate his son's return. That is unconditional love.

Why is God's unconditional love not only the greatest thing imaginable, but also the hardest thing for us to accept? We tell our kids before they go to sleep, "God loves you, and so do I!" We have bumper stickers that announce to all passing traffic, "God loves you." We even have posters with yellow smiley faces that say, "Smile, God loves you." That's all pretty unconditional. But then, like the Pharisees in Jesus' day, we tack on 613 additional things we think we have to do in order to merit God's favor and earn his love. Unconditional love with a boatload of conditions—maybe we keep saying, "God loves you" all the time because we're still trying to convince ourselves.

What Shane said to me that day in Las Vegas exposed the consequences of an unspoken belief of mine. I had grown up reading the Bible as an endless list of Thou Shalts and Thou Shalt Nots, and that approach had hindered my ability to see God's love as anything other than conditional. Unwittingly, I had come to believe that everything hinged on my perfor- mance and on my obedience to God's rules and regulations.

No matter how hard I worked and how often I succeeded at achieving my goals, I always felt that there was something more I could have done. Prayed for fifteen minutes? Twenty would have been better. Read a chapter in the Bible? Read the entire book next time! No matter how much I did, it was never enough to make me feel God's acceptance. There was always room for improvement. It was as if I assumed God was looking over my shoulder saying, "C'mon, Rusty, you can do better than that!" I know I'm not alone in feeling this way.

I remember a young man named Scott, who was in his midtwenties when we met. He was fresh out of college and climbing the tech-industry ladder. He'd grown up in the South, where going to church on Sunday is as normal as watching football on Saturday. Scott's parents had set a good example for him and taught him right from wrong, and he made great, God-honoring choices throughout his adolescence. When he went off to college and faced all the worldly temptations on campus, he remained faithful to the principles he'd been taught at home. After graduation, he set about establishing a life for himself, and that life included God.

Scott was very involved in our church's young-adult program. I watched him facilitate small groups, lead mission trips, and mentor the sons of single moms in our congregation. To everyone who knew him, he was an exemplary leader. But not to himself. I remember taking Scott out to lunch to thank him for all he'd done for our ministry. He looked back at me with exhausted eyes and said, "Well, I wish I could do more."

You could almost see the fear and insecurity in his eyes, and I tried to put him at ease with a little bit of joking. "Scott, you're already doing everything possible. I have no other jobs for you."

This didn't seem to help.

"I know," he said, "but it just seems I could do more. Maybe if I quit my job and came to work full-time at the church . . . then I'd be able to accomplish more for God."

I didn't have the heart to tell him that working full-time at the church had yet to satisfy my quest to "do enough."

Occasionally, when Scott and I would have lunch, his voice would begin to tremble as he discussed all the things he wished he could do for the church and for God. But time just didn't permit. This created a strange undercurrent of guilt in his life. More than once he asked me about Jesus' command to the rich young ruler to sell all he had and give it to the poor.[1] Scott couldn't help but think that maybe he *was* that rich young ruler. Should he sell everything he had? He'd often point to the passage in James that speaks of "pure and genuine religion" as "caring for orphans and widows in their distress."[2] Should he volunteer more at the local hospital or take in some foster children? He was unable to experience the joy in what he was doing for God because of regret for what he couldn't do. No matter how much I talked about the grace and love of God, he wasn't buying it. Perhaps it was because he sensed my hesitancy to trust in it myself, but it was probably more because he and I faced similar roadblocks to getting to the truth about God's love.

I grew up in a Midwestern town nestled in the buckle of the Bible Belt, where church attendance not only was normal but also seemed required. My parents were first-generation Christians, so they did as they were told after they were baptized: They were in church every time the doors were open. I can remember going to church every Sunday as a child dressed in a white suit with white shoes and carrying a white Bible. I was a Whirlybird, a Jet Cadet for Jesus, and I even did a stint in Bible Bowl. When I moved on to junior high, I added Sunday-night youth group, Wednesday-night prayer meeting, and Tuesday-night door-to-door calling. It's safe to say that my parents burned up a lot of tire tread driving back and forth from church, and I'm grateful that they did. At church, I was introduced to biblical teaching three times a week, built lifelong friendships, and found mentoring that encouraged me to go into ministry. But growing up with such a regimented schedule and already being a people pleaser who likes systems, I became convinced somewhere along the way that God's love for me depended on my performance for him.

> I became convinced that God's love for me depended on my performance for him.

Whether you can relate to my upbringing or not, I've met many people during my years of ministry who believe, as I once did, that God's love is conditional rather than unconditional. Like me, they learned to think of the Bible as a list of rules that must be obeyed, simply to avoid negative consequences. If I don't sin too much, then I won't go to hell. If I go to church enough, then God will tolerate me a little longer. Or the classic one I grew up with: "If I don't drink, smoke, or chew . . . or go with girls that do . . . then God will be happy with me." While this way of thinking may keep us out of trouble, it also leads to a life of insecurity, spiritual workaholism, and a constant fear: *What if I go one sin too far?*

The Thou Shalts

Whether you've spent much time in church or not, you are probably very familiar with the phrase "thou shalt not," which forms the backbone of the Ten Commandments in the King James Version of the Bible.[3] These were the standards that God set in place to define how his people would relate to him and to each other. Yet as clear-cut and basic as these commandments were, people felt the need to add to them.

The practice of adding conditions began soon after the Ten Commandments were established. In an effort to make sure the Jewish people kept the original ten, religious leaders began to add additional precepts to create a protective barrier: If you don't break the precepts, then you won't break the commandments. But over time the precepts became more than suggestions; they became laws of their own by which the people were judged and condemned—as much as if they had broken the original, God-given Ten Commandments.

By the time Jesus arrived, more than 613 additional precepts had been developed. Talk about a good idea gone bad! And then one day, one of the scribes asked Jesus to pick his favorite:

One of the teachers of religious law was standing
there listening to the debate [between Jesus and the
Sadducees]. He realized that Jesus had answered
well, so he asked, "Of all the commandments, which
is the most important?"[4]

You can almost hear the antagonism in his words. Standing
in front of a crowd, this man was trying to make a name
for himself. He was trying to get Jesus to put his foot in his
mouth and appear to be a heretic in the eyes of the law. But,
as always, Jesus' reply was both brilliant and simple:

The most important commandment is this: "Listen,
O Israel! The LORD our God is the one and only
LORD. And you must love the LORD your God with
all your heart, all your soul, all your mind, and all
your strength." The second is equally important:
"Love your neighbor as yourself." No other
commandment is greater than these.[5]

Straight from the lips of the Lord himself—that should
settle it, right? But after Jesus ascended into heaven, it didn't
take long for his followers to start adding to his words. This
behavior did not appear only among the Pharisees. You can
trace it throughout church history, from the institution of
penance, to the selling of indulgences, to disagreements
about baptism and the proper way to take Communion, to
all the rules and regulations that govern the thousands of

denominations that have sprung up, to all the expectations (spoken and unspoken) that complicate our relationships in the church and the world. We have a habit of setting up extra rules and laws when it comes to connecting with God, and it lures us into believing that these rules determine God's favor in our lives.

I grew up in a church that preached the Bible . . . and a little extra. Not only were we not supposed to break the Ten Commandments, but we also had a few additional things enforced to help keep us on the straight and narrow. For instance, R-rated movies were forbidden, and even PG was suspect. Dancing was also off-limits, for fear it would lead to *touching*, which could lead to the

> We have a habit of setting up extra rules and laws when it comes to connecting with God.

condemnable offense of "heavy petting"—a phrase I've heard only in church youth groups. As for music, the piano and the organ were the only acceptable instruments on church property. On one occasion, our church hosted a concert by a very popular Christian group. The assumption was that they would come in and simply sing their songs. Instead, to the elders' surprise and chagrin, they brought guitars, drums, smoke machines, and lights. I distinctly recall hearing one of the elders say to my parents after it was all over, "Next time we let anyone sing on our stage, we'll make sure they are Christians!" Yep, we put the "fun" in fundamentalism.

As much as I now laugh about some of these additional

Thou Shalt Nots, other churches were even more strict. Some forbade watching TV; others called card playing a sin; and for others, ginger ale was off-limits because it might appear to be champagne. My home church may have been on the liberal side!

For every Thou Shalt Not limitation on our actions, there were just as many Thou Shalts telling us what we ought to do. Thou shalt be in church every time the doors are open. Thou shalt serve your time in the nursery or teach Sunday school. Thou shalt help out with all church work days. Thou shalt invite all your neighbors to church every Sunday. Thou shalt read your Bible every day—even the difficult parts of the Old Testament.

I'm not disparaging the Ten Commandments—or serving at church or reading the Bible—but not every instruction from God is a Thou Shalt. When we treat his instructions as if they are, we can end up living with feelings of guilt and shame for all the times when we don't obey, and with feelings of pride when we do. It seems that the more we focus on Thou Shalts, the more we notice people who don't—which can make us even more prideful. But God hasn't called us to a regimen of regulations. He wants to engage with us in a living *relationship* and to partner with us in accomplishing his purpose and plan in the world. When we reduce our Christian faith to rule keeping and other performance-based measures—such as how often we attend church, how often we pray or read the Bible, or how many friends and neighbors we've invited to Sunday services—we can start to believe that it's *our* responsibility to change the world *for* God and then present it to him as a gift in the hope that he'll say, "Well done, my good and faithful servant."

The problem with seeing God's words as a series of Thou Shalt commands is that we find it nearly impossible to believe that God's love could be anything other than conditional.

> We can start to believe that it's our responsibility to change the world for God and then present it to him as a gift.

The Never Minds

The flip side to a Thou Shalt approach to faith is what I call a Never Mind mind-set, which sees much of what is in the Bible as outdated and obsolete—archaic laws that no longer apply to us.

God gave his people three types of laws in the Old Testament: *moral*, *ceremonial*, and *civil*. The moral laws are encapsulated in the Ten Commandments. The ceremonial laws were meant to regulate how the people worshiped through Temple presentation and animal sacrifices. The civil laws dictated Israel's hygienic, dietary, and judicial rules. Through these laws, God not only revealed himself to his people but also protected them from harm in a time when disease, infection, and malnutrition were common.

Now that we live in a different time, we tend to see these laws as outdated. After centuries of progress in hygiene and food preparation, we don't struggle with the same health issues that a nomadic society in 1500 BC would have lived with. Spiritually, because of what Jesus did on the cross, we don't have the same need for sacrifices and Temple procedures. As Hebrews 10:18 says, the final sacrifice has been made: "When sins have been forgiven, there is no need to offer any more sacrifices."

But here is the struggle we face: Now that our sins have been forgiven, what do we do with all the other commands in Scripture? Our tendency is to try to keep most of the moral laws but regard everything else, such as the ancient ceremonial and civil laws, as obsolete. For many, these biblical laws have become mere suggestions or are so archaic that they think God would say, "Never mind."

When we encounter a biblical principle that makes us uncomfortable—such as God's instructions on the giving of tithes and offerings—we simply say, "That's under the old law." Or if we find ourselves on the wrong side of the warnings against divorce and adultery, we say, "We're under God's grace." But how do we regard the admonition to act justly, love mercy, and walk humbly with our God? Do we see it simply as good advice?

When we assume that the grace of God not only cleanses us from our sin but also lets us off the hook for all acts of disobedience, we cheapen the authority of God in our lives. He begins to seem like the parents with two unruly kids I saw recently at a restaurant. The young boys, probably three and five years old, had taken the entire place hostage with their antics—climbing over the back of the booth and roaming the aisles between tables, staring at the people who were trying to enjoy their meals. The parents had nothing but empty warnings and threats in their arsenal: "If you don't sit down, you won't get any dessert." But the kids were unfazed. And sure enough, when dessert time arrived, both kids got their treat.

If we see the Bible as an ancient book filled with Never Minds, it can lead us to reckless choices, as it did for the early church in Rome. Look at how Paul addresses this problem: "Well then, should we keep on sinning so that God can show us more and more of his wonderful grace? Of course not! Since we have died to sin, how can we continue to live in it?"[6]

If we start picking and choosing which parts of the Bible to obey, we risk overlooking God's loving wisdom and warnings that are designed to protect us and minimize the pain of this life.

I saw this in Emma's story. Sometime during her high school days, she decided to chart her own course far away from God. She ran away for a few years, spent some time in Las Vegas, made money any way she could, and eventually came back home with a baby. Much to her surprise, her parents welcomed her home with open arms. Their Sunday school class at church threw a welcome-home party that doubled as a baby shower. Emma was quick to embrace the forgiving and loving grace of God, and there was a noticeable effect on her life. She never missed church, she began volunteering in the student ministry, and she even began dating a great Christian young man. This formerly rebellious and obstinate teenager was transformed into a loving young adult. Her embittered face softened into a joyous smile, and her apprehensive spirit was replaced with a generous heart. Yet something was not quite right.

Though Emma was certainly an example of God's grace in action, she seemed to want to overlook the choices and circumstances that had gotten her into trouble. When she led a small group of younger teenage girls, she often ignored the instructions and warnings in Scripture in favor of citing verses such as 1 Peter 4:8—"love covers a multitude of sins"—and a modified version of Romans 8:28: "all things work together for good." After about a year, Emma's passion for her newfound faith began to wane. Despite her radical transformation and unbridled enthusiasm for God, she began to have doubts and serious questions about God. When she and her boyfriend split up, it wasn't long before Emma walked away from the church again.

The problem with seeing God's blessings as unconditional is that we assume he is obligated to do what we say, give us what we ask, and change our world—with or without our participation. This not only can lead to a lack of respect for God and his holiness but also can undermine our shallow faith when God chooses to say *no*. We assume that his gentle and loving rejection of our request is a harsh and unreasonable rejection of us.

When God is silent, we assume he's not listening.

When God says *wait*, we hear it as disapproval.

When God says *not yet*, we think he is unkind.

When the church confronts sin, we say, "Judge not!"

When we read a *no* in the Bible, we say, "You can't take everything literally" and "Maybe that doesn't apply to us today."

When we read a command in the Old Testament, we say, "That's the old law. We're saved by grace."

When our focus is on God's *obligation* to his nature of grace and forgiveness, we can overlook our *responsibility* in partnering with him.

One of the most popular passages in the Bible is one of the most often misunderstood because of a case of the Never Minds. In Romans 8:28 Paul writes, "We know that God causes everything to work together for the good of those who love God and are called according to his purpose for them."

We love the phrase "God causes everything to work together for good." We use this liberally, in any situation. During the real estate bust in Southern California and the great recession when families were losing their homes, it was common to hear of people who had disregarded biblical wisdom, and even common financial wisdom, to get into houses they could not afford. When the bank came calling, their anger turned toward God: "Why is he not working everything together for my good?" Clearly their view of "their good" was not the same as God's. I've seen parents who indulge their kids with credit cards, cars, and permissive attitudes, enabling these kids to get into serious trouble. And when that trouble comes home to roost, their response is, "Why is God not working everything together for my good?" The Never Minds cause us to embrace the promise without the premise.

The startling truth in Romans 8:28 is that God's promise is not for everyone. We often overlook the last part of this verse: ". . . for the good of those who love God and are called according to his purpose for them." God brings good out of situations to those who love him and are part of his mission. In other words, for those who are in *partnership* with him.

> God brings good out of situations to those who love him and . . . who are in partnership with him.

When all of God's Word becomes Never Minds, obedience becomes optional and blessings are viewed as unconditional. When we think blessings are unconditional, we become entitled. This leads only to frustration and disappointment when God is seemingly silent, leading us to believe that he doesn't love us.

Unconditional Love, Conditional Blessings

How can we live in the tension of unconditional love with conditional blessings? I caught a glimpse of how this can work in the life of a self-proclaimed ragamuffin.

I was at a ministry conference in Dallas, perusing the schedule of afternoon classes. After a strong recommendation from a friend, I slipped into a hotel ballroom to hear an old Irish Catholic author named Brennan Manning. Though others appeared to know who he was, he was new to me. I found myself compelled by every word he said. I'm not sure how old he was at the time (he has since passed away), but the years had been hard on him. His short stature, weathered face, snow-white hair, and deep smoker's voice told a story of a difficult road of faith. On top of that, he randomly shouted and swore.

Who was this guy?

Manning told his story—a story filled with abuse, divorce, alcoholism, and guilt. I've heard people tell these kinds of stories before, but they usually end with getting saved, changing their ways, and riding off into the sunset with Jesus happily ever after. But Brennan Manning's story didn't seem to have any happy resolution. He was very much in the thick of his struggle with sin and shame. And yet he was overwhelmingly convinced that Jesus loved him—not as he should be, but as he was. I believed him. Manning had found a way to live in grace yet walk in obedience. He lived life in partnership with God, even though he occasionally stumbled.

Afterward, I thought, *I gotta find out if this guy is even real.* I went up to the front to see whether I could meet him. I waited in a long line as he graciously, yet seemingly painfully, spoke to everyone. When he finally got to me, I didn't even know where to begin. How do you say, "You've helped answer some of the biggest mysteries in my life," without sounding like a stalker? I just looked at him, shook his hand, and said with tear-filled eyes, "Thank you."

Perhaps you've experienced the consequences of Thou Shalt living, and you know what it's like to live believing that God's love is conditional.

Perhaps you've experienced the results of seeing the Bible, or at least parts of it, as a big Never Mind. You know the feeling that God, at times, has left the room and left you on your own. This can feel like freedom . . . until you need him.

Over the next few chapters we're going to walk through some of the most liberating, empowering, and freeing opportunities God has given us. These are not opportunities for us to try to earn his love. And they are not opportunities for him to earn ours. They are God's great invitation for us to partner with him. But before we can truly partner with God, we have to resolve in our own hearts the issue of his love for us.

chapter three:

WHEN YOU TRUST GOD'S LOVE,
THEN GOD WILL INVITE YOU
TO PARTNER WITH HIM

As you can imagine, discovering I didn't believe that God loved me put my faith in a bit of a tailspin. What do you do when you're a pastor, whose job is to tell people about the love of God, but you're not sure whether it applies to you? I wish I could say that all I had to do was tell myself, "God loves you, Rusty, so now get on with your life." But I couldn't. It wasn't that simple. This realization sent me in pursuit of *anything* that could fix things for me.

I spent a lot of time asking other people, from other pastors to new Christians, about God's love. I listened to their stories with great interest. Many of the new Christians talked about their newfound faith in Jesus with such enthusiasm and joy that I couldn't help but be intrigued. Still, when they would describe how the love of God had enfolded them in a time of need, or the sense that Jesus was holding them came in the midst of their pain, there was a part of me that thought, *Really?*

During weekly services at our church, we often show prerecorded testimonies of people who have recently come to faith. While most people in the congregation would applaud and sometimes weep after hearing the stories of people who'd had miraculous Jesus moments, I felt skeptical—and then I felt guilty. Was I the only one who felt this way? Were these experiences available to everyone but me?

As a kid, I watched the TV show *The Incredible Hulk*. It was a rather sappy rendition of the comic-book hero and the pain behind his anger. In case you were watching *Dallas* during those years instead of this fine program, I'll give you a quick synopsis.

Dr. David Banner (played by Bill Bixby) loses his family in a car accident when he is unable to rescue his wife because of a lack of strength. He then spends years researching similar stories that had different outcomes—stories in which people had achieved superhuman strength to move massive objects in order to save lives.

"Why couldn't I do that?" he wonders. Soon he is asking, "What do I have to do to be able to do that?" This leads to a scientific experiment involving gamma rays that leaves him with a rather angry alter ego—the Hulk, played by body-builder Lou Ferrigno—and an apparently endless supply of purple pants.

As I talked to various people about their faith, I felt like David Banner: researching others' stories while wondering, *Why not me?*

My questioning led me to ask other pastors whether they had ever felt as I did. I found that many were just as frustrated as I was. I heard stories of burnout, trust issues, a lack of intimacy, and a constant feeling that God was disappointed in them—or worse, *mad* at them. It was as if we were all crossing our fingers, hoping that God's love as described for others was good for us as well.

I also spent time putting the story of my life on paper to see all the peaks and valleys. The goal was to see God's presence and provision in all these moments. But for every moment that some would identify as an experience of God's presence, I found an easy way to explain it away. Yes, God might have been there, but I'm sure he was disappointed that he had to bail me out one more time.

"Do You Trust God?"

Finally, my journey led me to a Christian psychologist, Dr. John Walker of Blessing Ranch Ministries, who lived and worked at that time in the mountains of Colorado. My wife and I flew into Denver, rented a car, and began the long drive north on I-25. We drove until we nearly reached Wyoming, all the while wondering whether we were going the right way. *Is there even anything out here?*

Eventually, we found it: a beautiful ranch, secluded from the rest of the world, that served as a retreat and counseling center for pastors and their families. We were scheduled to be there for a week, and though I was hopeful it would help, I was not optimistic.

A month before our visit, in preparation for this week, I had purchased a journal at Barnes & Noble and sat down to write out everything I was thinking about God. The journal filled up quickly with words that described distance, fear, and anxiety in my relationship with God and thus in my relationships with other people as well. Now, standing in the lobby of the ranch building, the day had come to share my journal—my life—with Dr. Walker.

He invited Lorrie and me into his office. It was pretty much what I had expected: full bookshelves along the walls, a large desk in the middle of the room, across from which were two chairs and a coffee table with a box of tissues—standard issue for a therapist's office. Dr. Walker started with some brief getting-to-know-you questions and wrote down everything I said.

I answered his questions, but I was anxious to get into my journal. I wanted to be fixed quickly, and there was no need to waste time.

Just give me a few tips to remedy how I feel, and we'll get out of here.

When the time came, I started reading him my journal. He listened intently, and even took notes, but Dr. Walker was not in a hurry. After I read several pages, he motioned for me to stop. Looking across the desk at me, he asked a question that caught me off guard.

"Do you trust God?"

"Sure."

I felt that was the right answer, especially for a pastor. But Dr. Walker wasn't settling for one-word answers.

"We all say we trust God, Rusty, but trust isn't yes or no. Trust is a pie that is cut into several slices. We typically trust God with only a few of those slices, and we all keep at least one slice—and maybe more—to ourselves. There are some things that we just aren't sure we can entrust to God."

I was puzzled at first. But he was right.[1]

What slice are you keeping back?

Maybe it has to do with your health. You wouldn't say you're a hypochondriac, but you've been known to troll

WebMD at the sight of a freckle. On Facebook, you've cyber-stalked people you don't even know just to read about their symptoms or a diagnosis they received. You find yourself fretting about diseases you might get. You try to pray about it, but can God really be trusted with your health? After all, you know good Christians who have died at an early age.

Maybe your slice of the trust pie is your finances. You worry about money, get stressed about money, fight about money. You worry about what you have and what you don't have. You want to believe the pastor when he says, "Just pray and God will provide," but let's be honest: Christians around the world starve every day. Can you trust God with your finances?

Maybe your slice of the trust pie is your happiness. You'll go to church, read your Bible, and even pray; but when it comes to your three inalienable rights—life, liberty, and the pursuit of happiness—you'll take care of the planning. You tend to think, *It makes me happy, and surely God wants me to be happy.* You might ask God to bless your attempts at happiness, but at the end of the day you think, *If it's meant to be, it's up to me.*

> For the past twenty-five years, my approach to my relationship with God had been to try to prove my worth.

As Dr. Walker said, we all have at least one slice of the trust pie that we keep to ourselves. In my case, I realized I had trusted God with the church, my family, and our finances. But I didn't trust him with *me*.

At this point, I had a major breakthrough. For the past

twenty-five years, my approach to my relationship with God had been to try to prove my worth. Yet this was in stark contradiction to the promises recorded in Scripture. God vows to love us, to never leave or forsake us, to forgive us and forget our sins, to work in and through our lives, and to be with us forever. I believed this on behalf of everyone else but only gave lip service to it for myself. When God said, "When you jump . . . then I'll catch you," my response was, "I think I'll just stay here on the deck."

For the first time, I realized my problem was not that others had experienced things with God that I hadn't. My problem wasn't with what God had done or not done in my past. My problem was that there was a disconnect between what I *knew* and what I actually *believed*—between my mind and my emotions. I was struggling with what to do with the facts and with my feelings. This is a common hurdle that many people must cross. Do we let the facts determine our feelings, or do our feelings determine our understanding of the facts?

We all have feelings that don't line up with the facts. I may feel that I can eat a box of Krispy Kreme doughnuts and not suffer any adverse effects, but the fact is that those doughnuts will give me a sugar rush that will leave me curled up on the floor in the fetal position. I may feel that I can play point guard for the Los Angeles Lakers, but the facts paint a different picture. Feelings aren't the same as facts, but feelings can greatly influence our perception of the facts.

We see this in the life of Thomas, one of Jesus' twelve

disciples. Here was a guy who had gone all-in and put his trust in Jesus. For three years he had followed Jesus, watching him perform miracles and hearing him talk about the coming Kingdom of God. And Thomas believed it all: Jesus was the Messiah, the Son of God, and Thomas had gotten in on the ground floor of this world-changing movement.

Then suddenly, it was over. Jesus was crucified, and the dream was gone. Everything Thomas had believed now seemed to be a fallacy. And when the other disciples received word that Jesus had returned from the dead, Thomas was nowhere to be found. The wild ride was over for him.

When the disciples finally saw Thomas again, they told him, "Jesus is alive!" But Thomas replied, "I won't believe it until I see the nail prints." In other words, "Fool me once, shame on you. Fool me twice, shame on me!"

History gave Thomas an unfortunate nickname— Doubting Thomas—but he was only doing what we all do: letting his feelings determine his view of the facts.

When it comes to faith, most people whom I've observed do the same as Thomas. I know; I was one of them. In my case, God's unconditional love seemed too good to be true. Because I *felt* that God didn't love me, I assumed it had to be a fact. But why would I take that approach to my faith when I didn't think like that in any other area of my life? Imagine if we allowed our feelings to define our under-standing of the law of gravity. Being lighthearted, I might feel that I can fly. But if I try it, I won't be touching the sky. Fact is, I'll be touching the pavement—with my chin.

For years I had allowed my feelings to define my understanding of the facts about God's love for me. But now I could see that a better approach was just the opposite: I should allow my understanding of the facts to positively affect my feelings. Consequently, my biblically based understanding that God loves me unconditionally and has only my best interests at heart could and *should* result in an emotional reservoir full of good and positive feelings.

> I had allowed my feelings to define my understanding of the facts about God's love for me.

After my meeting with Dr. Walker, I decided I had to get back to the facts and allow them to change my feelings and emotions about God. I spent some time alone with the Scriptures, reading the truth about God as if for the first time. I went through the Bible and read every passage that talked about the love of God, until it suddenly hit me: What would happen if I took God at his word? What would happen if I took seriously what God says about his love for me? What if I let *his* facts determine *my* feelings, rather than allowing my feelings about him to define my understanding of him? I finally said to myself, *What do I have to lose?*

I wish I could say that I instantly and miraculously understood the depths of God's love for me, but that's not how faith works. Growth is a process that takes time. I did, however, begin to see that, in his love, God was calling me—as he calls all of us—to a spiritual *partnership*. That was a key piece I had been missing for years.

Our Partnership with God

In the book of Philippians, the apostle Paul writes, "Work hard to show the results of your salvation, obeying God with deep reverence and fear. For God is working in you, giving you the desire and the power to do what pleases him."[2]

In other words, in our "partnership in the gospel,"[3] we have our part and God has his. It's not *only* his responsibility, and it's not *only* ours: It's truly a partnership. God has a plan for our lives, but we have to participate.

What I've discovered is that *when* we partner with God to change the world, *then* he partners with us to change our lives. God loves us unconditionally— and there is nothing we can do that will make him love us any more or any less—but when it

> When we partner with God to change the world, then he partners with us to change our lives.

comes to his blessings and our role in our partnership with him, we live in a *When/Then* world. *When* we surrender to God's will and obey his commands, *then* he empowers us to work according to his purpose for us.

This pattern goes all the way back to the Garden of Eden. When God created the world, he placed the first man and woman in an amazing paradise, where they would find meaningful work and enjoy friendship with God. But God gave Adam a specific When/Then warning: When *you show your obedience by avoiding this one particular tree,* then *our great relationship will remain unhindered and uninterrupted. When you daily choose to obey me, then there will be nothing to separate us. We will continue to enjoy a deep and rich friendship; we will walk together, live together, and enjoy creation together. But if you eat from the forbidden tree, you are choosing your ways over mine and deciding to disobey me. You will experience guilt and shame, and you will fracture not only our relationship but all other relationships to come. Your soul will be disconnected from me, and you will surely die.* From the beginning, God established the conditional boundaries in his *when/then* creation.

This pattern continued in God's relationship with the children of Israel. After four hundred years of slavery, he sent Moses to deliver his people from the grip of the Egyptians. God then began the most awe-inspiring and terrifying display of power the world had seen since the Flood. Over the course of several months, he afflicted the land of Egypt with ten plagues that included blood, darkness, insects, and eventually death.

Overwhelmed by the power of the God they served, his people stumbled out into the desert to a newfound freedom. Can you imagine the questions they must have had? *Who is this God? And why is he protecting us?*

As God began to reestablish the boundaries of his relationship with the nation of Israel, he gave them another When/Then statement:

If you will listen carefully to the voice of the LORD
your God and do what is right in his sight, obeying

his commands and keeping all his decrees, then I will not make you suffer any of the diseases I sent on the Egyptians; for I am the LORD who heals you.[4]

Just as God did with his first children (Adam and Eve), he now did with the children of Israel. He told them, "*When* you obey me, *then* it will go well for you. I will protect you; I will provide for you; I will lead you into a land filled with prosperity. *When* you show obedience to me, *then* my long arm, which you saw extended on Egypt, will be used to defeat your enemies."

When the obedience of the children of Israel proved to be short-lived, *then* God began to administer his corrective justice on them. For the next five hundred years, the people experienced an ongoing cycle: disobedience; then destruction; then repentance, deliverance, and restoration; then forgetfulness and further disobedience. Finally, in a heart-to-heart dialogue with King Solomon after the completion of the Temple in Jerusalem, God gave another When/Then promise: "If my people who are called by my name will humble themselves and pray and seek my face and turn from their wicked ways, I will hear from heaven and will forgive their sins and restore their land."[5]

I remember a time when my wife and I sent one of our daughters to her room for throwing a fit. We made it very clear to her that all she had to do in order to come out of her room was stop her tantrum and say she was sorry. That was all. No extra chores, no time in the boo box, no need to copy a sentence one thousand times. Just stop acting up and say you're sorry.

But her fit continued.

Lorrie and I waited patiently by the door, mumbling under our breath, "*When* you stop and say you're sorry, *then* you can come out . . . *then* the day can continue . . . *then* we can have a great time tonight. *Just stop and say you're sorry!*"

When I read 2 Chronicles 7:14, I can almost hear God's parental tone. It's almost as if he's standing outside Israel's door, saying, "Just stop it and say you're sorry! When you humble yourself, then I will pour out so many blessings on you that you won't know what to do with them all. I made you for relationship—now let's get back to that!"

When/Then thinking does not end with the Old Testament. Jesus carried on the same teaching. He often said things such as "When you've seen me, then you have seen the Father"[6] or "*When* you believe, *then* you will see God's glory."[7] In fact, every beatitude in the Sermon on the Mount has a When/Then undertone. When we are poor in spirit, then we will receive the Kingdom of Heaven. When we mourn, then we will be comforted. When we hunger and thirst for righteousness, then we will be filled.

If we live in a When/Then world, wouldn't it make sense that it was created by a When/Then creator? And if we read a When/Then Bible, wouldn't it make sense that it was written by a When/Then author? In addition to the Thou Shalts, and beyond the Never Minds, lies a way to live that allows us to partner with God in his When/Then world.

When I present these ideas to people, I sometimes meet with resistance. Let's explore some reasons why some people hesitate to embrace a When/Then God.

"That sounds like a works-based theology!"

For some people, hearing that God will respond in a particular way when we do something sounds like a works-based plan of salvation. In other words, *when* we do enough good works, *then* God will save us. But that's not the case at all. Our good works can bring God's blessing into our lives, but our salvation is purely by grace and grace alone. That's why grace is so amazing. Once we discover the magnitude of our sin and acknowledge the penalty that is due, we are stunned to realize that Jesus stepped in and absorbed the *then* for our *when*. Grace is God's way of interrupting this natural flow in order to extend salvation to us.

Paul emphasizes this truth in his letter to the Ephesians: "God saved you by his grace when you believed. And you can't take credit for this; it is a gift from God. Salvation is not a reward for the good things we have done, so none of us can boast about it."[8]

God's grace has saved us, and it's not a reward—it's a gift. But this in no way diminishes the truth that God uses a When/Then approach to pour out his blessings. In fact, the very act of receiving God's grace is based on a When/Then premise: "If you openly declare that Jesus is Lord and believe in your heart that God raised him from the dead, you will be saved."[9]

God still moves in certain ways when we partner with him. We still live in a When/Then world created by a When/Then God.

"That sounds like karma!"

Unfortunately, when it comes to spirituality, some Christians shy away from When/Then thinking because it sounds to them too much like karma—the cause-and-effect philosophy rooted in Buddhism and Hinduism. Through karma (which means *action*), good or selfless actions lead to good consequences, whereas bad, evil, or selfish actions lead to bad consequences. Karma is a cumulative measure that can affect one's destiny in successive lifetimes. If you do enough bad, you might be reincarnated as a goat. One view of karma suggests that we should avoid helping a homeless man by the side of the road because he has earned his place in life through his actions (karma) and now must pay for it. God's version of When/Then would say that we are to be a blessing to the less fortunate, and that in blessing others we ourselves are blessed. Karma is based on our own efforts. God's version of When/Then is based on his power working through us. Karma is based on "so that"—I do good *so that* I will be given good things. But Christianity is a "because of" way of life—our motivation always begins with God. We love *because* God first loved us. We serve *because* God serves. We forgive *because* God has forgiven. When/Then is an outgrowth of God's love, not something we must do to receive God's love.

"That sounds like a prosperity gospel!"

Because of my upbringing, I often hesitate to talk about God's blessings for fear of straying into a prosperity gospel or "health and wealth" theology. I don't ever want to suggest that if you just have enough faith, you'll never get sick or bounce a check. Just like everyone else, good and faithful Christians still experience loss, poverty, and disease. As Jesus himself said, God "causes his sun to rise on the evil and the good, and sends rain on the righteous and the unrighteous."[10] But we can also make the opposite mistake, saying that blessings will come only in heaven and that we should simply grin and bear it through this life.

I had to go all the way to Uganda to learn the difference. Several years ago, during a building campaign, our church decided to tithe from our campaign funds. We designated our money to go toward building orphanages in a poverty-stricken and war-scorched area of Uganda. By partnering with a great organization, we were able to connect with a local church and sponsor some of the children there. Later, our board of elders traveled to Uganda to see the results. While we were there, I met some of the most remarkable people I've ever encountered. They told us their stories of growing up in wartime Uganda, witnessing the murder of their parents, fearing for their own lives, and facing homelessness and starvation. But then the orphanage rescued them. Despite all the horrific things they had endured, their story was punctuated by an ongoing list of blessings from God.

They could not stop quoting Scripture, singing praises, and talking about God's goodness. In fact, I never once heard the question, "Why do bad things happen to good people?" I was humbled by their faith and reminded that God's blessings are not always health, wealth, and the avoidance of pain, but rather joy, peace, contentment, love, and so much more.

The Bible is filled with When/Then statements about how to unleash all of God's blessings in our lives. The truth is that, every time I read the Bible, I'm reminded that God doesn't have a problem talking about blessings—including health and wealth. In fact, it seems that God has a virtual store-room full of blessings he is just waiting to pour out on us. He wants to overwhelm us with his gifts of presence, help, comfort, direction, contentment, freedom, and wisdom, to name just a few. Though God's blessings are available to us, I fear that many of us will never access them because we're too busy telling ourselves and others, in so many words, "God is good, but don't get your hopes up!"

> The Bible is filled with When/Then statements about how to unleash all of God's blessings in our lives.

Even though people have used the When/Then principle to induce a guilt trip in themselves or others, to try to earn their salvation, or even to try to manipulate God, they don't negate the daily evidence that we live in a When/Then world. The misuse of God's When/Then principles doesn't mean they shouldn't be used at all. We shy away from words such as *consequences*, *works*, and *blessings*; but if we skip over God's When/Then statements in the Bible, we risk missing out on God's purpose and plan for us.

This is where *partnership* comes into play.

When we view God's commands as Thou Shalts, we see them as impossible tasks, and we resent having to work for such an unreasonable God.

When we view God's words as Never Minds, we assume that God is working for us like some cosmic genie of grace, and we resent him when we don't get what we want.

But when we view God's words as When/Thens, we see our relationship with him as a *partnership* in which we get to work with God in his rescue mission for the world.

We live in a When/Then world, created by a When/Then God, who offers us a chance to participate with him in his mission to change the entire world—not just our world. Up until now, you may have been operating in your own strength, trying to do everything for God; or you may have been expecting him to do everything for you. What I want to suggest is that God may be saying, "Why don't we do this together?"

I can tell you from personal experience how this works. Discovering the biblical language of When/Then helped me not only to partner with God but also to climb out of a very dark place. In the following chapters, I want to share some of the When/Then principles that I have found to be the most helpful.

> God offers us a chance to participate with him in his mission to change the entire world.

chapter four:

WHEN YOU

WALK WITH JESUS,

THEN GOD WILL

HELP YOU LOOK

LIKE JESUS

I once gave Jesus money to get to Vegas.

Granted, it wasn't actually Jesus—his name was Mason, and he had been coming to our church off and on for about a year—but occasionally he would show up dressed like Jesus. It helped that he had flowing, sandy brown hair, and his scruffy beard made the resemblance even more convincing. But when he donned the robe and sandals, he took it to another level. Even for California, it was something to behold. I always enjoyed seeing people's reactions—and I suppose Mason did, too. Some thought he was kidding, others thought he was part of a skit for the children's ministry, and I'm sure that at least a few assumed he was the church mascot. I had to draw the line when someone asked him to turn their Evian into merlot. (Kidding.)

Though Mason certainly looked the part, his character and the decisions he made did not match his appearance. He had divorced his wife and left her with their children—for no reason other than needing his freedom. One Sunday we found him on the street corner outside our building, picketing the church. He carried a sign that read, "The tithe is only in the Old Testament." I'm sure that most people who drove by had no idea what he was protesting. One of our pastors went out and talked to Mason and found him to be amicable. He put down the sign, came inside, and had some coffee and doughnuts (which I've found cures a lot of problems).

The last time I saw Mason and his Jesus costume was the day he arrived at church in an RV he'd purchased for a few hundred dollars. The vehicle was held together with duct tape and superglue, but it ran. He said he was heading to Vegas but needed some money for gas. This was one of those benevolence requests that we decided didn't require a reason or an explanation. We simply handed him some gas money and prayed for "traveling mercies."

As he drove away, it occurred to me that looking like Jesus means so much more than simply dressing like him. Likewise, looking like Jesus means so much more than merely dressing like a Christian.

In some social circles, dressing like a Christian means dressing up for church. My friend Mike Breaux tells the story of being in a Golden Corral restaurant years ago on a Sunday afternoon. He was in line at the salad bar when he heard someone yelling a few tables away. Looking around, he noticed a man in a suit that was covered in Thousand Island salad dressing. And not just a little bit, either. It was all over the man's face, suit, tie, and shoes. A young waitress was handing him paper towels and apologizing profusely. Apparently she had tripped on her way to refill the dressing on the salad bar and had launched the contents of a five-gallon bucket all over this poor man.

His response was something less than gracious. In a tirade laced with words that would scorch your grandmother's ears, this man—and his wife, I might add—was hollering for all to hear: "This was a brand-new suit and now it's ruined! How could you be so clumsy? I want to see the manager!"

By this point, the ruckus had already brought the manager

to the scene. He apologized and promised to pay for the suit to be dry-cleaned, but the man wouldn't have it. He wanted a *check* for his brand-new suit. The interesting part is that this happened on a Sunday afternoon. Why would a guy be wearing a suit on a Sunday afternoon? He had probably just come from hearing a great sermon on forgiveness or on loving your neighbor as yourself.

My friends in the food service industry say that the worst day of the week to wait tables is Sunday. Not because business is slow—on the contrary, business is booming. What makes it a terrible day are the hundreds of people who stream in right after church, wearing their Sunday best but displaying their personal worst. They are rude to the waitstaff, critical of the menu, make a mess of the table and its surroundings, and then leave a generous 1-percent tip—or worse, leave only a religious pamphlet telling the waiter why he or she is going to hell. It's no wonder people don't want to come to church.

We've all seen examples of people who look like Christians but don't act like Jesus, whether it was the person in front of you in line at the returns counter berating the clerk for some deficiency with a product, the church softball team whose language made you cover your kids' ears, or the guy with the fish symbol on the back of his car who gave you the one-finger wave in traffic. We've all seen it. Truth is, we've probably all been that person at one time or

> We've all seen examples of people who look like Christians but don't act like Jesus.

another. It takes more than a big leather Bible and a WWJD bracelet to make us look like Jesus.

The apostle Paul gives us a great picture of what it means to truly look like Jesus. It comes from the inside and shows itself as the *fruit* that our lives produce. "The fruit of the Spirit is love, joy, peace, patience, kindness, goodness, faithfulness, gentleness, self-control; against such things there is no law."[1]

In John 15:5, Jesus says, "I am the vine; you are the branches. Those who remain in me, and I in them, will produce much fruit." Those who remain in Jesus (some translations say *abide*) will produce the natural fruit of the vine, which includes all the good qualities that Paul mentions. For anyone who looks, the branches are one and the same with the vine. That's what it means to look like Jesus. When the Spirit of God is in us and we partner with him, we begin to see the overflow of his presence in our lives. It means that we actually begin to *think* and *act* as Jesus would if he were visibly present.

Who wouldn't want to have all these things in their lives? We'd all like to have more joy—not just happiness, which comes and goes, but deep, soul-filling joy. In the midst of all our anxiety, confusion, decisions, and deadlines, who wouldn't like to have more peace? And everyone else in our lives would certainly appreciate it if we had more patience.

So if it's at least possible for us to think and act more like Jesus, how do we do it?

Is Transformation Possible?

For those of us who lean toward the Thou Shalt way of living, we assume that if we're going to look like Jesus, it's all on us. In a word, it's all about *willpower*. We just need to work harder. We just need to try harder. We just need to read the Bible more, pray more, go to church more, and maybe even fast. Then, we think, we'll look like Jesus.

Though it may be true that reading the Bible, going to church, and praying can help us grow closer to God, if those practices become our primary focus, we can be lured into thinking that we can produce the fruit of the Spirit on our own. Not only that, but we become achievement oriented, believing that if we just do what the Bible says, we'll become pleasing to God. And when we don't do what the Bible says, we see ourselves as failures.

Willpower is another term for self-help. If you think about it, most self-help books are about ways to achieve the things on Paul's list in Galatians 5: how to get rich (peace), how to relax and enjoy life (joy), how to affair-proof your marriage (love). On and on it goes.

For those of us who lean toward the Never Mind philosophy, we assume that if we're going to look like Jesus, he'll make it happen. Almost like surprise plastic surgery, we'll wake up one morning and see Jesus in the mirror.

Think about the ways we put the entire onus on God. Your wife has another come-to-Jesus meeting with you about your temper, to which you respond, "Be patient, God isn't finished with me yet."

"But you've been a Christian for forty years! Is God waiting for a building permit from the city so he can start this renovation project?"

Maybe the issue is with an addiction. You may be an alcoholic who keeps stopping in at the bar "just to say hi" to your friends. Or maybe you're an overeater who keeps buying Double Stuf Oreos. Or you struggle with inappropriate websites but haven't gotten around to setting up filters on your Internet service. And when you stumble you think, *God should be making this easier for me.*

I, for one, struggle with impatience. I've been known to yell at my family to get in the car so we can race to the beach and relax. Yes, I realize there's something a bit counterproductive about shouting, "Hurry up and enjoy yourself!" I finally realized that I was waiting for God to wave the magic wand and turn me into a laid-back, tea-sipping, it's-all-good hippy. But that wasn't happening.

Team Transformation

The Bible speaks of transformation not as a Thou Shalt or a Never Mind but as a When/Then. God really promotes *teamwork* in the area of transforming us to look more like Jesus.

Think about the metaphor that Paul uses to describe the desired result. *Fruit.* Well, how do we get fruit? We grow it, right?

Maybe not.

The truth is, none of us has ever grown anything. At best, we've produced the *conditions* for growth—bringing together good dirt, good seeds, plenty of water, and lots of sunlight. (None of which we've created, by the way.) Then nature takes it from there. The same is true with the fruit of the Spirit. We can bring about the conditions for growth, but it's God who generates the increase.

> God really promotes teamwork in the area of transforming us to look more like Jesus.

Paul is hardly the only person in the Bible to describe life with God this way. Psalm 1 opens with a similar image: "The one . . . whose delight is in the law of the LORD, and who meditates on his law day and night . . . is like a tree planted by streams of water, which yields its fruit in season."[2]

The psalmist suggests that there are two basic ways to spend our time here on earth: either rejecting God's plans for us or partnering with God to see those plans come to fruition. If we do things God's way, listen to God's words, and align ourselves with them, then we grow—like fruitful trees planted along a riverbank.

As with Paul's description of the fruit of the Spirit, we aren't given credit for producing the fruit, but we are called to create the conditions for that fruit to be produced.

We hear something similar from the prophet Jeremiah, who draws a contrast between the willpower approach—trusting in our own strength and wisdom—and trusting in God.

This is what the Lord says:
"Cursed are those who put their trust in mere humans,
  who rely on human strength
  and turn their hearts away from the Lord.
They are like stunted shrubs in the desert,
  with no hope for the future.
They will live in the barren wilderness,
  in an uninhabited salty land.
But blessed are those who trust in the Lord
  and have made the Lord their hope and confidence.
They are like trees planted along a riverbank,
  with roots that reach deep into the water.
Such trees are not bothered by the heat
  or worried by long months of drought.
Their leaves stay green,
  and they never stop producing fruit."[3]

Not only does God say that people who place their confidence in him will be "like trees planted along a riverbank," he adds that these trees "are not bothered by the heat or worried by long months of drought. Their leaves stay green, and they never stop producing fruit." In other words, no matter how many threats we face, life flows within us, and we continually bear fruit. In contrast, Jeremiah says that people who trust in themselves and turn away from partnership with God will be "like stunted shrubs in the desert, . . . in the barren wilderness, in an uninhabited salty land." Who wants to be a stunted shrub?

Among the many passages that picture people as flowers and trees, none is more poignant than the words of Jesus in John 15, where he explains that he is the true vine and we are the branches.

Before we look at the text in greater depth, let's picture the scene. In his Gospel, John is telling Jesus' life story, so of course things slow down the closer we get to the end. By chapter 15 in John's account, Jesus has already turned water into wine, brought sight to the blind, and fed thousands of people by miraculously multiplying a little kid's sack lunch. Very soon he will be arrested in the middle of the night, and he'll watch as his closest friends run away or deny him. Then he'll stand trial before the most powerful men in the land and be put to death on a cross.

But before Jesus completes his mission on earth, he has a few things to say to his followers. Before he moves onward toward the Cross, he stops for a few on-the-go teaching moments. Many Bible experts call John 14–17 Jesus' farewell address because this is the last time he slows down long enough to teach an extended lesson. For some reason, John is the only Gospel writer who records this teaching. Because he was there when it happened, there must have been something about either the content or the tone of Jesus' words that he still remembered decades later when he wrote his account of Jesus' life.

I am the true grapevine, and my Father is the gardener. He cuts off every branch of mine that

doesn't produce fruit, and he prunes the branches
that do bear fruit so they will produce even more.
You have already been pruned and purified by the
message I have given you. Remain in me, and I will
remain in you. For a branch cannot produce fruit if
it is severed from the vine, and you cannot be fruitful
unless you remain in me.

Yes, I am the vine; you are the branches. Those
who remain in me, and I in them, will produce
much fruit. For apart from me you can do nothing.
Anyone who does not remain in me is thrown away
like a useless branch and withers. Such branches are
gathered into a pile to be burned. But if you remain
in me and my words remain in you, you may ask for
anything you want, and it will be granted! When you
produce much fruit, you are my true disciples. This
brings great glory to my Father.

I have loved you even as the Father has loved
me. Remain in my love. When you obey my
commandments, you remain in my love, just as I obey
my Father's commandments and remain in his love.
I have told you these things so that you will be filled
with my joy. Yes, your joy will overflow! This is my
commandment: Love each other in the same way I
have loved you. There is no greater love than to lay
down one's life for one's friends. You are my friends if
you do what I command. I no longer call you slaves,
because a master doesn't confide in his slaves. Now you

are my friends, since I have told you everything the Father told me. You didn't choose me. I chose you. I appointed you to go and produce lasting fruit, so that the Father will give you whatever you ask for, using my name. This is my command: Love each other.[4]

For Jesus, the topics of *remaining*, *loving*, and *being fruitful* were clearly on his short list of "things I must tell you before I go." When you know you're about to die, you don't waste words.

There's a lot going on here, but the point is actually pretty simple: *We should stay connected to Jesus so that we come to reflect his way of life.* Jesus gives us a metaphorical image and then fleshes out the implications of that image with a few commands.

> Unconnected from the vine, a branch is no longer a branch. It becomes a *stick*.

First, the metaphor: Jesus is the vine, the Father is the vinedresser, and we are the branches. You'd be hard pressed to find a better image to depict how we partner with God to bear fruit in our lives—fruit that reflects the character of Jesus. The importance of remaining in the vine is obvious. Branches don't produce their own life. Unconnected from the vine, a branch is no longer a branch. It becomes a *stick*.

For kids, sticks are great for pretend sword fights and make-believe magic. For adults, sticks are good for burning. Sticks burn quite well, actually, because they're dead. They've been cut off from their natural life source, so they break and burn easily.

When we rely on our own strength and look within ourselves for the answers to life, we're like sailboats on a windless morning or computers that aren't plugged in or sticks that are lying on the ground. On our own, we are no more likely to thrive spiritually than a stick is likely to produce flowers or fruit. It won't happen.

Jesus said, "Apart from me you can do *nothing*."[5] Branches must stay attached to the vine because only the vine can provide the never-ending stream of necessities in order to produce blossoms and bear fruit.

Jesus' disciples should have known this already. They were part of God's people, and this was hardly the first time God had used vine imagery to refer to his people. Jesus, in his final discourse, borrowed the image from Psalm 80 and Isaiah 5, among other places.

Psalm 80 is sung from exile, after God judged his people's sin by allowing them to be taken captive by a pagan empire. The psalmist refers back to the Exodus as a time when God "brought us from Egypt like a grapevine . . . and transplanted us into [his] land" after driving out the pagan nations and clearing the ground.[6] In this new land, the vine prospered and grew:

We took root and filled the land.
Our shade covered the mountains;
    our branches covered the mighty cedars.

> We spread our branches west to the Mediterranean Sea;
> our shoots spread east to the Euphrates River.[7]

But that season of serenity has long since passed. Intruders and wild animals have stolen and destroyed the fruit, and the vine has been "chopped up and burned."[8]

The picture of the vineyard in Isaiah 5 is not any happier. This time, God is the one who sings the psalm. Like a jilted lover, he recalls his tender care for Israel against which the people have rebelled. God "looked for a crop of good grapes, but it yielded only bad fruit. . . . He looked for justice, but saw bloodshed; for righteousness, but heard cries of distress."[9]

So how does God respond?

> Now I will tell you
> what I am going to do to my vineyard:
> I will take away its hedge,
> and it will be destroyed;
> I will break down its wall,
> and it will be trampled.
> I will make it a wasteland,
> neither pruned nor cultivated,
> and briers and thorns will grow there.
> I will command the clouds
> not to rain on it.[10]

When Jesus came along saying, "I am the vine; you are the branches," these images of destruction were at least part of what would have come to the disciples' minds. As it turns out, Jesus' friendly little vineyard analogy has a sharp edge to it. Jesus may emphasize the positive aspects—the promise of fruitfulness for those who remain in him—but the promise comes with a warning: You can cut yourself off from the life of the vine by trying to figure things out on your own. The When/Then equation works both ways.

However, if a veiled warning was the only point that Jesus was trying to make, the usefulness of his words would be pretty limited. If we're trying to find the right road from St. Louis to Los Angeles, it's only marginally helpful for someone to tell us, "Don't go east." We need to know which road to take, not just which ones to avoid.

> You can cut yourself off from the life of the vine by trying to figure things out on your own.

This brings us to the necessary conditions for growth—which are all about *partnership*.

Jesus emphasizes the good that can happen if we will let it. The overarching call is clear: *remain*. Jesus uses the word ten times, mostly to make sure we know the benefits of abiding and the perils of not abiding.

What does it mean to remain in Jesus? Sometimes we can get a much clearer sense of what the Bible teaches by looking beyond our English translations to examine the words used in the original languages. But in this case, the underlying Greek word simply means *remain*, *abide*, or *stay*. If we want to produce fruit, we must stay close to Jesus, drawing our wisdom, strength, energy, and direction from him. We can't willingly disconnect ourselves or wander off. We must make the effort to stay put—intentionally and persistently.

This requirement would not have surprised Jesus' original disciples. They were, after all, *disciples*, a word that evokes images of a powerful person's followers; monks at the feet of a spiritual master; or Peter, James, and John tagging along with Jesus. But *disciple* simply means *follower*. Rabbis had apprentices: followers who studied the rabbi's particular interpretation of Scripture and sought to apply it to their own lives. But carpenters also had apprentices: students who watched how the master worked with wood and who took notes and imitated the master's work, so that they, too, might have a successful career. Simply put, a disciple is someone who *stays* with a teacher—watching, listening, absorbing, and imitating—so that one day the student might be just like the master.[11] That seems to me exactly what Jesus means with this image of vine and branches in John 15: *Stay with me, listen to me, and learn to be like me.*

I'm reminded of how the apostle John summarizes the call of Jesus on our lives:

> We can be sure that we know him if we obey his commandments. If someone claims, "I know God," but doesn't obey God's commandments, that person is a liar and is not living in the truth. But those who obey God's word truly show how completely they love him. That is how we know we are living in him.

Those who say they live in God should live their lives as Jesus did.[12]

There you have it. Obeying Jesus is the active version of "remaining in" Jesus. They are the same thing. If you remain with Jesus—that is, if you listen to what he says and do the kinds of things he does—then you will bear fruit. When you walk with Jesus, then you will (truly) look like Jesus.

> When you walk with Jesus, then you will (truly) look like Jesus.

Helpful? Yes, though still a bit vague. But if you look more closely at what Jesus says, you'll notice that he adds a bit of detail to what *remaining* is all about. He digs a little deeper into the concept of abiding by giving four supporting directives.

1. He tells us to *remain in his words.*

I'm amazed at how many sayings people attribute to Jesus that he never actually said. I've heard many modern-day clichés attributed to Jesus—everything from "God helps those who help themselves" to "Everything happens for a reason." If we don't know what Jesus actually said, it's not only easy to put words in his mouth but also nearly impossible to remain in his words.

Every once in a while, I have a conversation with someone who feels the need to let me know why he or she is considering leaving our church for another. Their discontentment often echoes a familiar theme: "We just aren't getting fed here."

This odd term is common among many Christians, but

I like to probe a little bit to find the underlying meaning. Often I'll ask some questions to expose some blind spots the person may have.

"Are you in one of the small-group Bible studies we offer?"

"Are you serving in any capacity?"

"Tell me about the friends you are bringing to church."

I find that interaction with other Christians, service to others, and outreach are key components of "getting fed."

At some point in the conversation, I will typically ask, "How long have you been a Christian?"

Just as typically, the person will look at me with pride and respond with "Fifteen years" or "Twenty years."

This is the point at which I calmly say, "It's time to feed yourself."

Remaining in the words of Jesus is not your pastor's responsibility, your parents' responsibility, or even your spouse's responsibility. It's *your* responsibility. God may use others to bring transformation to our lives, but we must do our part—and this starts with *knowing* and *doing* what he said.

For some, it works best to create a time and a place to sit down every day and read the Bible. They may use a reading plan, read a chapter a day, or use a devotional to guide their study.

For those who find that too structured, I have found that memorizing a verse in the morning and refreshing myself with it throughout the day can be very energizing. Another technique of mine is to jot down the words of Jesus on Post-it notes and place them around my house, car, and office. This provides a nonstructured way to tether my thoughts to his words throughout the day.

2. He calls us to *remember his words.*

Even if we know what Jesus said, we still must *remember* what he said in order to do it. That's what it means for his words to remain in us.

When my wife is preparing to make dinner, she'll sometimes send me to the grocery store for a few items that we're missing. If this were our big grocery run for the week, I'd probably be inclined to make a list. But for only five or six items, I usually feel that I can remember. But many distractions can occur between my house and the store. If I'm not careful, I'll end up wandering the aisles and talking to myself: "What did she say she needed?"

My solution is to repeat the list over and over again on my way to the store. I find I'm much more likely to do what my wife has asked when I remember what she said.

3. He calls us to *obey his words.*

Even when I successfully remember what my wife asked me to get at the store, I still have to bring the right items home. Changing my mind at the last minute about what I'd rather have for dinner is not an option. My wife created the menu. She made the list. I just follow the list.

Beginning to look like Jesus requires us to carry out his commands. When I take a mission trip, for example, I'm obeying Jesus' call to "go into all the world."[13] When I spend time with my kids and teach them about Jesus, I'm obeying

Jesus' call to draw kids to him. When I give of my resources to others, I'm obeying Jesus' directive to be generous. These items may not have been on a menu that I selected, but that isn't my job. I just fulfill the list. And when I do, I become more like Jesus.

4. He instructs us to *love one another*.

So many of Jesus' commands revolve around how we are to love one another. Sometimes this "one another" is someone I don't know. He might be a homeless person on the street corner, or she could be my server at a restaurant. Either way, when I show an act of love through a gift, a tip, a kind spirit, or even a prayer, I become more like Jesus.

Sometimes the people who are the hardest to love are the ones I know best or am related to. It might be a friend against whom I'm holding a grudge or a family that left my church because they weren't being fed. Either way, when I extend forgiveness and grace, I become more like Jesus.

It's not hard to see how all of these things fit together. And it's not hard to see how obeying the words of Jesus creates a type of teamwork with God that transforms us into people who look like Jesus.

Pastor Chad Moore once said, "Someone is always rubbing off on you." That's true of both good company and bad company. If you stay close enough to Jesus, he will be the one influencing you. Stop relying on your own willpower to try to change yourself. Stop waiting for God to use a magic wand to turn you into someone who looks like Jesus. Partner with him. Stay close to him. Let him rub off on you.

Remain in Jesus and walk day by day with him, and you will become like "a tree planted by streams of water, which yields its fruit in season and whose leaf does not wither."[14]

Who wants to be a stick?

chapter five:
when you relax, *then God will guide you*

Hi, my name is Rusty, and I'm a worrier.

I have been a worrier for as long as I can remember—going back to those sleepless nights over something we were making in my kindergarten art class. Don't laugh. Weaving a basket from strips of colored paper is a daunting task when you're five.

Somewhere around second grade, I had a brief stay in the hospital due to an ulcer. Too much stress from playing third base on the T-ball team, I guess.

Though I learned to manage my anxiety as I got older, it was still an issue in high school and beyond. Asking a girl out on a date usually required a roll of Tums. Playing on the basketball team was great—until game day. And when I decided to introduce myself to the young woman at college who would one day become my wife, it took me two years to get up the courage.

Part of this I justify by saying, "It's just my personality." I'm a little high strung and have a touch of OCD. I'm not a Nervous Nellie; I'm just a little bit tense. I'm not worried; I'm just concerned. I don't like surprises, so I play out the worst-case scenarios in my mind. That way I'm prepared, whatever happens.

My dad also had an ulcer, so apparently the tendency to worry runs in the family. And now it seems that I've passed it on to my kids.

One night when Lindsey was eight, she called me back into her room about thirty minutes after she'd gone to bed.

When I came in from the hallway, it was clear she had something heavy on her mind. I pushed aside her stuffed animals, sat down on the edge of the bed, and asked her what was wrong. It was hard to see the emotion on her face because the only light in the room was from the fish tank, but the fear in her voice was unmistakable.

"Sometimes I lie in bed and worry about you or mom dying," she said.

Whoa. This was no kindergarten craft project she was worrying about.

My mind began to race. *When did this begin? Where did she get this idea? Is she going to be like me?*

Once I gathered my wits, I had to decide what to say.

Option A: *Avoid it!* "No one is going to die, honey. Everything is fine and always will be. Your life will be filled with smiles and rainbows, puppies and princesses!" But that seemed a bit much.

Option B: *Get real!* "You're right, Lindsey—everyone is going to die someday. I'm going to die, you're going to die. . . . In fact, let me tell you about what I just saw on the news tonight." That seemed like too much as well.

Finally a verse came to mind—something I had memorized years ago in an effort to deal with my own anxiety. I said, "Lindsey, let me teach you a verse. To understand it, we're going to pretend we are fishing. The verse says, 'Cast all your fears into God's mighty hand . . . because he cares for you.'[1] So let's put all our fears in our hand and pretend we are casting, just as you do when you go fishing with Grandpa."

One by one we put her fears in her hand and cast them into the mighty hands of God.

As I left Lindsey's room that night, I had mixed emotions. I felt pleased that the conversation had gone well. It seemed like a win in the "be a good parent" column. But I also felt conflicted. Because even as I taught my daughter that verse, I still struggled to apply it myself. My own "fishing style" functioned as if I were using a rubber band in place of the fishing line. I would cast my cares to God, but then they'd come snapping back at me—right between the eyes.

Throughout Scripture, God admonishes us against worry. Again and again he tells us to let him deal with it.[2]

If anyone in the Bible wrestled with anxiety and worry, surely it was Peter. He dealt with the guilt of denying Jesus; he faced death on a daily basis as an apostle in the early, persecuted church; and he stood before thousands and preached the gospel. Yet it's Peter who tells us to cast all of our fears into God's mighty hand.

> He tells us to be anxious about nothing but to pray about everything, and God will grant us peace.

Paul, too, dealt with fear and worry. He had to deal with his guilt over all the Christians he had seen killed; he lived with an ailment he referred to as a thorn in his side; and he spent countless days in prison because of the gospel. He also stood before kings and rulers and declared who the real king was. Yet he tells us to be anxious about nothing but to pray about everything, and God will grant us peace.[3]

Even Jesus addressed the subject of worry.[4] He reminds us that the flowers and the birds don't worry, and our heavenly Father loves us even more than he loves them. So we shouldn't worry either!

I agree with all this, but I still struggle with it.

Who Is Responsible for the Future?

One perspective is to believe that it is *our* responsibility to make the most of what we've been given. The book of Proverbs is filled with wisdom about working hard and preparing for the future.

Those who work their land will have abundant food.[5]

All hard work brings a profit.[6]

Do not love sleep or you will grow poor;
     stay awake and you will have food to spare.[7]

When I read these verses, I think: *Work hard and don't be lazy. Trust God as if it all depends on him, but work as if it all depends on me.* So I feel as if I have some responsibility in the matter of preparing for my future. I don't want the Master to return and find that I was a poor steward of his resources.[8] I want to be a worker worthy of my wages. I want to be wise with planning and saving and managing all that God has entrusted to me. That includes my money, talents, opportunities, resources, family, and time.

But there's a catch.

When I believe that preparing for the future and honoring God with my life is all my responsibility, I end up working, planning, preparing, saving . . . and bracing myself for what comes next as I worry that all my efforts will not be enough to satisfy God's expectations. In all my efforts, I rely less and less on *him*, and I worry more and more about *myself*.

The alternative is to assume that all the responsibility for my life lies with God. If he feeds the birds and clothes the flowers, why would I not just expect him to take care of me, as well? I have been amazed at the number of times I have heard this perspective from people whom our church has helped to walk through unemployment and homelessness. They know enough of the Bible to quote the verses about not worrying and letting God meet their every need. They know the words of Jesus concerning flowers and sparrows, and thus they assume that God will swoop in with a lottery check—or at least a job. (And not just *any* job, but something in management with a corner office and a reserved parking spot.) There have been times when I've asked people, "Where have you applied for work?" and they've said, "Nowhere—I'm just praying that God will have someone contact me." But what seems to be faith often leads to their blaming God when he doesn't bring the miracle they are trusting in. This is not partnership with God.

Most people know that there is a balance between working hard and trusting God. But how do we find that balance? And how do we keep from letting our concern about the future consume our present?

Facing the Future Together

In the Sermon on the Mount, when Jesus talks about the birds and the flowers, he invites us into a partnership with God that will free us from worry. Far from being a mere pep talk—"Don't worry! Be happy!"—this passage of Scripture is packed with reasons why we don't have to worry.

Matthew sets the stage for us in chapter 4 when he says that Jesus began teaching, "Repent, for the kingdom of heaven has come near."[9] Here we see the overall theme of Jesus' ministry: *establishing God's heavenly Kingdom here on earth*. That doesn't mean everything will magically fix itself. But it does mean that a new way of living is possible. Contrary to the popular assumption that *repentance* means little more than feeling really bad about the really bad things we've done, the word actually calls for a new mind-set. In Matthew 5–7, Jesus unpacks what this new Kingdom mind-set is all about. But if you blink, you might miss the critical connection between his earlier statement about repentance and his subsequent command against worry.

> Repentance is not just leaving behind our sins; it also means leaving behind our desire to control everything.

Repentance is not just leaving behind our sins; it also means leaving behind our desire to control everything. Repentance means letting go of our need to always be perfect, our need for everyone else to be perfect, and our need for everything in our lives to work out perfectly.

When we give those responsibilities back to God, we stop worrying.

Now here's an important distinction that I don't want you to miss. When I said in chapter 2 that a Thou Shalt approach to faith is a faulty way of understanding our relationship with God, I did not mean to suggest that God's commands are somehow invalid. If they were, we'd all find ourselves in the Never Mind camp, right? So as much as we want to avoid falling into the trap of a performance-based, Thou Shalt mind-set, we cannot overlook the fact that Jesus' admonition to us to abstain from worry is an actual command. In fact, Jesus commands his followers twice in Matthew 6, "Do not worry."[10]

To be honest, I could handle this better if it were merely a suggestion: "You know, guys, you might not want to worry so much." It makes perfect sense to me as advice—like the kind of advice I'd rather give to others than follow myself. But a command? It seems a little unrealistic. Do not worry—*at all*? It seems to put the onus back on me, but it doesn't. The key to understanding biblical commands is to remember that every command points beyond itself to the God who gave it. And the God who has given us these commands is operating from a heart of pure love that has only our best interests in view.

Here is an easy formula for how to understand God's commands (or laws): First, we must dig beneath the *precept* to find the underlying *principle*, and then dig a little deeper to discover how it all points to the *person* of God.

Let me give you an example. The Bible says, "You shall

not murder."[11] The principle behind this precept is that life is valuable and we should not end someone's life just because we want that person eliminated. This principle points to the fact that God is the one who gives life and takes it away.

Here's another example: The Bible says, "Never stop praying."[12] The principle behind this precept is that the circumstances of life should not determine whether we talk to God. The person behind this principle is God, who is equally sovereign in good times and bad.

Now let's apply the same line of thinking to the command not to worry.

Do not worry about your life, what you will eat or drink; or about your body, what you will wear. Is not life more than food, and the body more than clothes? Look at the birds of the air; they do not sow or reap or store away in barns, and yet your heavenly Father feeds them. Are you not much more valuable than they? Can any one of you by worrying add a single hour to your life?

And why do you worry about clothes? See how the flowers of the field grow. They do not labor or spin. Yet I tell you that not even Solomon in all his splendor was dressed like one of these. If that is how God clothes the grass of the field, which is here today and tomorrow is thrown into the fire, will he not much more clothe you—you of little faith? So do not worry, saying, "What shall we eat?" or "What

shall we drink?" or "What shall we wear?" For the
pagans run after all these things, and your heavenly
Father knows that you need them. But seek first his
kingdom and his righteousness, and all these things
will be given to you as well. Therefore do not worry
about tomorrow, for tomorrow will worry about itself.
Each day has enough trouble of its own.[13]

The precept is clear: *Do not worry.*

Here's the principle behind the precept: *God will provide.*
What is it about the person of God that anchors our trust?
Jesus tells us two important things about God here: *God is our
Father*, and *God has what it takes to provide for us.*

First, Jesus calls God "your heavenly Father." In fact,
Jesus refers to God as "Father" fifteen times in the Sermon
on the Mount—and *fifty* times during his farewell address
in John 14–17. Do you think he's trying to make a point?

In the story I told at the beginning of the chapter, Lindsey
eventually went to sleep that night. Why? In part, perhaps,
because she understood what I told her about casting her
cares into the hands of God. But let's be honest: She was
eight, so the real reason was that her daddy had come into her
room and assured her that everything would be okay.

But what if she understood how inadequate I feel as a
parent much of the time? And what if she understood that I
really have no control over the life-and-death issues she was
worried about? I told you that I'm a worrier, and worriers like
me need something more than sentimentality if we're going

to relax. So after Jesus describes God as our Father, he continues with an illustration of just how powerful our Father is. In a series of descriptions that have come to be known as the "omnis," Jesus portrays God as *omnipotent*, *omniscient*, and *omnibenevolent*.

To say that God is omnipotent, or all-powerful, means that he is more than capable of providing for everything within his good creation—the birds, the flowers, and you and me.

When Jesus describes God as omniscient, it means that he is all-knowing. This means we don't ever have to worry that God lacks the necessary information or wisdom to care for us. He's not an undereducated psychologist or a doctor who slept through one too many exams. He knows everything about everything, which means he knows everything about *you*.

Omnibenevolent, which means all-loving, might be the goofiest of the omni- words, but it's also the one we most fear isn't true. So what if God has all the power and all the wisdom? If he keeps it to himself, what good is it to me? But Jesus is quick to assure us: "Your heavenly Father . . . will certainly care for you . . . and he will give you everything you need."

When Jesus commands us not to worry, we can rest assured that his precept is rooted in the clearest possible picture of God. The underlying principle is that God will provide what

> When Jesus commands us not to worry, we can rest assured that his precept is rooted in the clearest possible picture of God.

we need so we can accomplish what he put us on earth to do. When we relax and trust him, he provides for us and directs our future.

God is not interested in having us follow rules for their own sake. He wants us to know him, love him, and live accordingly. And he is a God who says, "You can trust me with your future." He is the kind of author we can depend on to finish the story well. He is the kind of strong person who will catch us when we fall. His dependable hands enable us to relax and stop trying to control everything—or *anything*, for that matter! God says, "When you relax, then I will guide you."

Yes, but . . .

Even though I understand that God is my heavenly Father—and even though I grasp the importance of his omnipotence, omniscience, and omnibenevolence—I still have trouble trusting him at times. I still battle with him for control. I still wrestle with his will versus mine. And it still isn't easy for me to truly relax and allow God to take charge. I still have a few arguments left.

Argument 1: "I'm not worried . . . I'm just concerned!"

Have you ever said that? I'm not worried about my relationship with my kids—I'm only concerned that they will move away to college and never come home again. I'm not worried about dying—I'm only concerned that I might have that rare disease I saw on WebMD. I'm not worried about disasters—I'm only concerned that an earthquake will swallow us up at night.

There is a difference between concern and worry. Concern focuses on things that probably *will* happen, and it produces preventive or corrective action. Worry focuses on uncontrollable events and produces inaction. Worry says, "What if . . . ?" Concern says, "What do we do now?" I've found that my concerns turn into worries when I try too hard to control circumstances that are out of my control.

Jesus uses birds to illustrate the difference between concern and worry. Some birds eat twice their weight a day, but have you ever seen a malnourished bird? No. You never look outside at night and see birds pacing on the overhead wires, eating Tums and complaining, "I don't know what we're going to eat tomorrow!" But you do see birds about the business of gathering seeds, grubs, and insects. Just as the birds flit about and gather what they need, our concern about food should lead us to work diligently, even as we trust God to provide. Worrying about food causes us to sit idly by and imagine going hungry. Concern for the future says that we work hard, save some of what we earn, have reasonable expectations, and trust God to meet our needs. Worry about the future has us sitting idle and envisioning all the bad that could happen to us.

Argument 2: "If I don't make it happen, it won't happen."
This renegade mentality—"If I don't *make* it happen, it won't happen"—usually starts with good intentions but ends in

disaster. Much of our worry results from the undue pressure we put on ourselves to perform. This leads to a hectic pace of life, long work hours, increased stress at home, a lack of trust within our families, and disrespect for our friendships.

As we drive home from church on Sunday afternoon after hearing an inspiring sermon, it's easy to vow that we will trust God with the upcoming week. By Monday, the thought of trusting God with our day turns into a fifty-fifty proposal. By Wednesday, we are consumed with our own agendas, and on Friday night we sit exhausted in the car on the ride home wondering where God was during our rough week.

It's one thing to be motivated to have a good work ethic, but it's something else entirely to believe that anything good in our lives is a result of our own effort. Jesus tells us in Matthew 6 that our heavenly Father can handle everything: The birds of the air are provided with great riches, and the flowers are adorned in splendor. Worry, in fact, is a direct indication that we don't believe God will provide for us as he said he would.

> Worry is a direct indication that we don't believe God will provide for us as he said he would.

When Jesus says, "And all these things will be given to you as well," he's not talking about anything extravagant. He's referring to food and clothing—that is, *necessities*. And he doesn't say, "Don't worry because everything will be fine," but rather "Each day has enough trouble of its own." He's not saying, "Don't worry, this is going to be easy and you'll have all the money and possessions you want" but rather "Trust me, I'm with you."

If you're wondering why some people appear to be trusting in God and yet still don't have their basic needs met, think of it like this: Imagine I give my older daughter one week's worth of lunch money to buy lunch for herself and her sister, only to find out on Friday that she kept all the money for herself and that my younger daughter has been unable to buy lunch all week. My younger daughter has not experienced my provision—though she trusted me for it—but the fault lies with the daughter who was given more than she needed and didn't share. Most of us have more than we need, yet we're quick to question or blame God for those who are starving around the world.

Argument 3: "God's idea of what I need doesn't match my idea of what I want!"

Sure, I believe that God can meet my needs, but will it be what I was expecting? My tendency is to worry about what he *might not* give me, instead of enjoying what he has already given me.

When it comes to trusting God to provide for my needs, take care of my life, and fix my problems, I know God *can*, but I don't know whether he *will*. Ever been there? Of course, we've all been there. Perhaps a better way to say it is this: "I know God can provide, but I don't know whether his idea of what I need will match my idea of what I want." So God and I have this ongoing argument.

He says, "Trust me."

I say, "I'd like to, but I'm not sure that you'll fix this the same way I would."

"Then I guess you'll have to trust that my way is best."

"What's that, God? . . . You're breaking up. . . . I must be having trouble with my cell service again."

"Mm-hmm."

> "I know God can provide, but I don't know whether his idea of what I need will match my idea of what I want."

When I was a nineteen-year-old college sophomore, I learned an important lesson about trusting that God's way is best. For a few weeks, I had been struggling with some odd symptoms of sickness—losing weight, being thirsty all the time, and not sleeping well. I was feeling pretty bad. One weekend while I was home, I went to our family physician for a checkup. He suggested that we draw some blood and run some tests. I headed back to school not really thinking much about it.

Four days later, my basketball coach pulled me out of class and told me that my parents were on their way to get me. I had been diagnosed with type 1 diabetes, and they wanted to admit me to the hospital back home. My mind flooded with questions and concerns: *I don't even know what diabetes is! Is it terminal? Is it curable? How do I treat it? Is it something I can just live with? What's next?*

I was nervous and most of all confused. Over the next few weeks, I got a crash course in how to live with diabetes. Yet through every conversation with the doctor and every lesson about treatment and management, I had a strange sense of peace. I knew I was not alone. And though I never dreamed that I would be diagnosed with a chronic illness or prepared for diabetes, God was prepared. I can see now how he walked with me through the early days of confusion and how he continues to walk with me today. Was I concerned? Yes. But when I decided to relax and trust him rather than worry, he proved to be faithful.

I guess this was most clear to me when I saw the opposite approach lived out. Part of being newly diagnosed with diabetes meant I had to spend time in a support group for diabetics. As I listened to other members of the group, I was less than encouraged.

"My life is over."

"I've just given up."

"I'm just going to eat what I want and hope for the best."

It was a clear indicator of what happens when we sense that control has been taken away from us and it seems all hope is lost. But instead of giving in to the downward pull of the group, I thought, *I can try to manage this on my own and be bitter at God and everyone, or I can choose to let God walk me through it.* Like a lot of people who live with a chronic illness or other difficult circumstances, I don't know why God chose to allow my life story to include diabetes; and yet I've learned to trust in his wisdom, even when I don't understand it.

The Priority of Our Devotion

How can we relax and trust that God is in control on a daily basis? The key, I've found, has to do with our *devotion*—that is, the priority of our commitments.

As a worrier who worries about worrying, here's what I've discovered: I only worry about things I'm devoted to.[14] On the flip side, I don't give much thought to things I'm not devoted to. Allow me to illustrate.

I'm a Los Angeles Lakers fan. Consequently, I don't worry about what the Washington Wizards are doing. No disrespect to the Wizards, but I don't check their scores, follow them in the standings, agonize over their season, or stress out about their draft position or their trades. But I do all those things for the Lakers.

> We may worry only about what we're devoted to, but what would happen if we changed our devotion?

I'm also devoted to my kids, and I worry about their grades, what schools they'll get into, and their future career prospects. But I don't worry about *your* kids' grades. I want nothing but the best for your kids, but I'm not calling you at 9:00 p.m. asking whether they've gotten their homework done. The reason is simple: I'm devoted to my kids and not to yours.

We may worry only about what we're devoted to, but what would happen if we changed our devotion? This is exactly what Jesus tells us to do in the Sermon on the Mount. This is the pivotal When/Then statement that undergirds everything else we'll explore in this book: *When you seek the Kingdom of God above all else and live righteously, then God will give you everything you need.*

Easy to grasp . . . easy to say . . . so hard to do.

We resist this When/Then equation because we're not so sure that God has our best interests in mind. So instead we stress out and worry about our own little kingdoms every day and occasionally show mild concern about God's Kingdom at church. Consequently, we live our days worried, stressed, frustrated, and lacking joy, hoping against hope—and sometimes praying—that things will work out for us. It's no coincidence that Jesus precedes his statement about priorities with a warning against worry.

Don't miss that part of Jesus' command. He doesn't say, "Don't worry—be happy!" He says, "Don't worry about your own problems; instead, seek what is good for God's Kingdom and watch while he takes care of everything else along the way." When we truly realize that God is so big, so beautiful, and so worthy, we will forget about our own concerns because we can't stop thinking about *his*. When we devote ourselves to the Kingdom of God, all our other worries melt away. It's not that we're no longer concerned, but we no longer have reason to worry. Our devotion is now to the Kingdom, and the Kingdom is well in hand. This is the kind of partnership that God desires to have with us.

When we're devoted first to God's Kingdom, we worry a

lot less. When we're devoted first to our *own* kingdoms, we worry a lot more.

I would estimate that 99 percent of my own worry is wrapped up in trying to control *my* kingdom: my stuff, my comfort, my success, my sense of approval, and my happiness. But when I change my devotion to focus on God's Kingdom, I not only worry a lot less but also see that he takes care of my kingdom as well.

I've also noticed that when I'm devoted first to God's Kingdom, I make better decisions. When I no longer weigh decisions based on how they will affect *me* but focus instead on what pleases the Lord, I stop taking the path of least resistance and start taking the path of maximum impact for God and his Kingdom.

One weekend at our church, I had the chance to interview former NBA star A. C. Green. A. C. is a bit of a legend here in Los Angeles because of his time playing with the Lakers. He won three championship rings and is considered the NBA's "Iron Man," having played in 1,192 consecutive games. Yet during his basketball career he became known as much for his integrity off the court as for his talent on the court. Though A. C. was a single guy living the life of an NBA star, he made a decision to remain celibate until marriage. He took a lot of heat from his teammates, and members of the media made jokes at his expense. But A. C. kept his commitment until he got married in 2002 at the age of thirty-eight. When I asked him about his decision to take a stand for abstinence, he said, "It really wasn't about taking a stand for abstinence. It was about seeking first the Kingdom of God. God said to wait, so I waited. It was that simple."

I guess it can be that simple. As my friend Mike Breaux likes to say, "Following Jesus isn't easy, but it's not complicated." When we decide to seek God first and foremost, the rest of our decisions become a lot simpler. Personally, I tend to worry less about things that are simple.

> When we decide to seek God first and foremost, the rest of our decisions become a lot simpler.

Many of the When/Then statements involve an element of sacrifice. I surrender what I want: my will, my desires—even my comfort, and certainly my kingdom. And though it may sound like a lot to give up, the reward is far greater in return.

chapter six

WHEN YOU NOTICE GOD, THEN GOD WILL REVEAL HIS PRESENCE

I had no idea that it was *that* kind of swimsuit. Honest.

When my wife Lorrie and I, along with our nine-month-old daughter, moved into our new neighborhood in Valencia, just north of Los Angeles, we were eager to settle in and get connected.[1] Our prayer was that we would build close friendships, our daughter would have other kids to play with as she grew up, and we'd have the opportunity to invite everyone to the church. When I heard there was a community pool, I thought, *What better way to meet the neighbors?*

Lorrie and I decided that Saturday would be our inaugural trip to the pool. Though our daughter, Lindsey, wasn't old enough to swim yet, she did have a swimsuit. Lorrie found her own suit in one of the clothing boxes from the move, but I couldn't find mine, so I had to take a trip to the mall.

It was already summer in California, and we soon discovered that most of the stores were pretty picked-over in the swimsuit department. We went from looking for the perfect suit to looking for *any* suit that would fit, until finally we found one. It was the only one left on the rack, and it was highway-construction-cone orange. But it was my size, so I bought it. We were all set for Saturday. Lasting friendships, playdates, and eternal destinies hung in the balance. It felt as if this might be the most important pool visit of our lives.

When Saturday finally rolled around, we decided to wait until the afternoon to make our debut at the pool. After all, we didn't want to appear too anxious. Finally, we loaded up the stroller with pool toys, towels, Lindsey, and enough sun-screen to protect an elephant, and we began our trek through the neighborhood.

The action at the pool was in full swing—people staking their claim to chairs, blowing up rafts, and enjoying coolers full of beverages. As we entered the gate, I sensed that this could be a divine appointment.

As Lorrie got our chairs and towels situated, I began to talk to a few people. Being a good dad, I slathered Lindsey with a layer of sunscreen, popped her into an inflatable duck, and took her out in the shallow end for a tour of the pool. We played for a while, and then Lorrie and I switched places. When I got out of the pool, I walked around and met several of my new neighbors. They were friendly, we had some good small talk, and it seemed that our initial foray into Southern California culture was a success. You might even say it was going swimmingly.

After a few trips around the perimeter of the pool, I decided to join my family back in the water. I sat down on the steps next to Lorrie and Lindsey while trying to commit to memory the names of the people I'd just met. As I began to share some of those names with Lorrie, I became aware of the horrified look on her face.

"What is that all over your suit?" she said.

"What are you talking about?"

When I glanced down, I noticed for the first time that the bright orange suit I had innocently purchased had bright blue images that appeared once the suit was wet. I wish I could tell you that they were crosses or doves or pictures of Jesus. But no, they were topless women.

I could only imagine the thoughts that had gone through people's minds when I introduced myself as the pastor of a new church called Real Life. Maybe they thought it was clothing-optional! I slipped out of the pool and covered myself in a towel. After that stunning revelation, we didn't stay much longer. As we were leaving, I wanted to tell everyone: "I swear . . . I had no idea it was *that* kind of swimsuit. I never saw anything on the tag that said, *Caution: pornographic when wet.*"

The truth is that, even if the swimsuit had come with a warning label, I probably wouldn't have noticed it. I'm often guilty of overlooking the details. This has led me to buy cars that turned out to be lemons. I've purchased items

> We can live in God's presence our entire lives and never really notice him.

online, only to find that I'd ordered the dollhouse size. We even bought a house one time only to learn that we'd actually purchased the one next door. Yes, it's true.[2]

We've all had experiences where we didn't read the fine print or didn't notice the details. We assume that something is going to be one way, only to discover later that it's another way. Maybe for you it was a car, a mattress, or an online purchase. Or maybe it was something much more costly— a retirement investment, a business partnership, or even a marriage. You just failed to notice what has now become very obvious, and you're paying the price.

Seeing God is like that. We can live in his presence our entire lives and never really notice him.

John tells us it was like this even for the disciples. They spent three years with Jesus. They had front-row seats for the Sermon on the Mount; they collected leftovers from the feeding of the five thousand; and they hid behind rocks when he cast the demons into the pigs, in the first recorded serving of deviled ham. And then Philip has the nerve to say to Jesus, "Lord, show us the Father."[3] Are you kidding me? I wonder whether Jesus wanted to laugh or cry.

"Don't you know me, Philip, even after I have been among you such a long time? Anyone who has seen me has seen the Father. How can you say, 'Show us the Father'?"[4]

As much as I want to pick on Philip, I probably would have said the same thing. I miss the evidence of God's presence every day. I once prayed for weeks that God would provide a favorable outcome to an upcoming tough conversation I was dreading. I was up all night, pacing the floor, lying prostrate on the ground, and asking for God's intervention. When I finally sat down with the person, everything went perfectly. Hearts were softened, our words were kind, truth prevailed, and we even hugged when it was over. But two weeks later, when I had another tough conversation coming up, I found myself wondering, *Will God show up?*

How ridiculous is that? Yet that's what we do, isn't it? It's hard enough to notice when God is at work, let alone remember it.

Do you find it hard to see God amid the craziness of

your busy life, between the carpools, the soccer practices, the homework projects, the commutes to work, and the daily wondering about what we should fix for dinner tonight? And that doesn't even account for your time spent on the job. It can be hard to see God, and the longer we go without noticing him, the easier it is to forget what he's like—or worse, to forget that he's even there.

When I pray, it sometimes seems as if my prayers don't get past the ceiling. It feels like I'm just talking to myself. Does God really hear me? Is anyone there? Is anyone listening?

> When I pray, it sometimes . . . feels like I'm just talking to myself. Does God really hear me?

As a child, I prayed a simple prayer: "God is great, God is good"—but is he? When I see all the calamities in the world and all the struggles in my own life, it's natural to wonder: *Is God not able to handle it, or is he just unwilling? Is God not great? Is he not good? What is he like?*

Is God still present? Maybe he just set everything into motion and then walked away. How do I know he's still around? What's he been doing since Creation? Is he even in close enough proximity to be interested in my life and make a difference?

Why would he care about me? I mean, in the big scheme of things, why would he be interested in my petty little problems when there is terrorism, famine, and disease wreaking havoc all across the globe?

Jesus said, "Anyone who has seen me has seen the Father."

But how many days can we go without noticing Jesus? Could it be that the reason we have so many questions about God is that we've just failed to notice him?

The Classic Frog in a Kettle

When our elder daughter, Lindsey, was six years old, she loved frogs. Whether it was Kermit the Frog, Michigan J. Frog, or any random stuffed-animal frog, she loved them all. Occasionally on daddy/daughter dates, I would take her to the pet store to look at the frogs. She was content to watch them for what seemed like hours.

"Daddy, look at how they jump!"

"Daddy, look at how they sit there and do nothing."

I was convinced she was destined for a career as a zoo-keeper, a wetlands biologist, or a pet store manager.

You know what happened next, right?

In a weak moment, my wife and I decided to buy Lindsey a frog. Nothing too exotic—just a dwarf frog that lived underwater in a small tank. This seemed like a harmless, easy-to-care-for pet for a six-year-old. Just keep the water clean, throw in some food on occasion, and enjoy.

The frog was very active, so Lindsey was inspired to name him Jumpy. Hours of watching Jumpy bounce about as if he were trying to escape brought us all great joy—especially Lindsey. One day, I came home from work to find that Jumpy's tank had been moved from Lindsey's room to the kitchen windowsill. I thought this was an odd spot for a pet frog, but I assumed the best. When I asked my wife about it, she said, "We thought Jumpy would like to see the sun."

Unfortunately, when I walked over and took a closer look, Jumpy no longer appeared very jumpy. I put my finger in the water and immediately knew what had happened. Not only had Jumpy spent the day enjoying the sun, he had also enjoyed all the comforts of a hot tub. Apparently, when you put a frog tank on a warm windowsill all day, then the water will get very warm! I could only imagine Jumpy's last thoughts: *Isn't the sun pretty today? Is it getting warm in here?*

RIP, Jumpy.

If we're not careful, we can end up like Jumpy—well, not floating on the surface of a frog tank, but certainly lulled to sleep by our culture, our daily routines, and life's demands. We can go through life unaware of our surroundings and unaware of how God is seeking to work through us to accomplish his plan and his purpose.

Can You Hear Me Now?

I don't know about you, but I'd like to see the Father. I'd like to know he's near. I'd like to sense his presence throughout the day, rather than feeling alone. I'd like to know his nature, rather than fearing his wrath. I'd like to trust in his grace, rather than relying on my own good works, such as they are.

When I read about Jesus, I get a sense of God's goodness and mercy. And when Jesus says, "Anyone who has seen me has seen the Father," I think, *Great! . . . But how do I do that?*

The problem is that I fail to see Jesus enough or understand his Father.

This is where my instincts and my upbringing tell me that it's all *my* responsibility. As if God were playing a game of cosmic hide-and-seek and it were up to me to find him. The frustration I sometimes feel makes me resonate with a line from the song "Smell the Color 9" by Chris Rice: "I would take 'no' for an answer, just to know I heard you speak."[5]

Of course, this searching for God is nothing new. Ever since the beginning of the church, people have been using every means necessary to try to see Jesus. The early church gave us the New Testament: a collection of eyewitness accounts of the life of Jesus and a selection of letters describing how to live as a community of believers. This book is our good news, our marching orders, and our code of living. Inspired by God and recorded by his servants, the Bible helps us to notice God.

Jesus gave us Communion as a way to remember him. Just before he died, he shared a very important final meal with his closest followers. The point of the meal was to allow Jesus to explain how all our hopes for freedom point to him. After explaining all this, Jesus told us to keep meeting and eating in a similar way so that we will remember who he is and what he came to do. That's a great way to notice Jesus.

But when we feel that the responsibility to find God is all on us, we tend to need more than just Communion, a church service, and the Bible. That's why, over the last two thousand years, the people of God have been adding details, customs, and rituals to help themselves visualize God. From saints to bishops to popes and pastors, we often hold up people as icons when we can't see God. From cathedrals to stained-glass windows, statues, and altars, we create sacred spaces to help us feel closer to God. And from cross earrings to necklaces to tattoos and bumper stickers, we fixate on images to help us remember Jesus.

Our quest to see God can lead to us trying to help him communicate with us. I had a friend years ago who liked to use a Bible-reading method I called Bible roulette. She'd ask God a question, flip open the Bible, put her finger down, and assume that the verse she was pointing to was God's answer. Sometimes it would make sense—other times not. What do you do when you ask God whether you should get married, and you read, "You must not cook a young goat in its mother's milk"?[6]

We also attempt to see God in less theatrical or demonstrative ways. Monks use solitude, and nuns sequester themselves. Some Christians use verses on their phones' lock screens, Christian music in their cars, and daily readings e-mailed to their inboxes. Though all of these techniques may have some value, they can also distract us from seeing that God wants to partner with us in helping us to see him.

Some of us prefer to put the onus entirely on God: *It's his responsibility to get our attention.* We'll just go about our daily lives, and if God wants to get us to Egypt, he can have our brothers sell us into slavery.[7] In other words, we'll wait until God decides to show up in some rather dramatic way. If not lightning or a burning bush, we'll settle for a loud voice or at least the image of Jesus on our grilled-cheese sandwiches.

Unfortunately, this passive approach leads to the "siren" theory of seeing God. When I was growing up in Kansas, we lived under constant threat of tornadoes, especially during the spring months. But even when the skies turned dark and the winds began to shift, everyone had a theory: "We'll take cover when we hear the sirens." We tend to do the same thing with God. Our lives may be falling apart, we may feel aimless and void, or we may be stuck in a rut, doing the same things over and over and expecting a different result; but we assume that if God has a better plan, he'll make it known. And he'll do so in a way that we can't miss.

> When we use our happiness as the barometer for God's movement in our lives, we are wide open for deception.

Putting it all on God also leads to the "happiness" theory—that is, "God wants me to be happy. If what I'm doing makes me happy and God hasn't stopped me yet . . ."

When we use our happiness as the barometer for God's movement in our lives, we are wide open for deception. We can trick ourselves into thinking that God says *yes* to our choices because we enjoy them and they make us happy— even though he says *no* to them in Scripture. From my observations, the most common occurrence of this upside-down way of thinking is in dying marriages. Even though God has clearly forbidden adultery, you'll hear people who are having an extramarital affair say, "I wasn't happy. But now I am. And God wants me to be happy."

I'm not sure that God cares about our happiness as much as we do. I do know that he wants us to be *holy*. And holiness has a better chance of getting us to happiness than happiness does of getting us to holiness.

Neither of these theories suggests a partnership with God. They both say, "I'll notice God when he does something worth noticing."

Ah, but he already has.

I've Been Here All Along

Most things can be found if we look hard enough or in the right place. When we lose our keys, we retrace our steps. Why? Because we assume the keys will be found someplace we have recently been. When we can't find our way to the store or to someone's house, we plug our destination into a smartphone and simply follow the directions. Why? Because the map app is the most reliable way to get where we're going.

But there are other things that can't simply be *found*. They must be *revealed*. In my own power, I often cannot discern what my wife thinks about some issue or problem. Mostly it's because I'm a guy and most issues don't seem to be a problem to me. Because of this, my wife must *reveal* the problem to me. Which she is happy to do!

The bad news about God is that he is not someone we can understand by natural ability or hard work alone. Though we may be very bright, even our intellect and curiosity have their limits. God must reveal himself, or he will forever remain unknown.

Thankfully, God is inclined to reveal himself.

One day, Abraham was going about his business, as he had for the previous seventy-five years. Then all of a sudden, he heard from God, who shared with him all sorts of wonderful blessings.

"You're going to be great. You're going to have a huge and lasting family. You're going to have vast property to enjoy. You're going to have influence far beyond your years on earth. As a matter of fact, everyone else who ever lives will be blessed because of your greatness."

Who wouldn't want God to say *that*?

But God had prefaced these blessings with a condition: "I want you to leave behind everything you've ever known. Leave your homeland, your community, and your father's household. Leave it all behind and go."[8]

And if that weren't drastic enough, God didn't even tell Abraham where he wanted him to go! Abraham was just supposed to start walking and assume he would hear from God along the way.[9]

God revealed himself, but it wasn't exactly cut and dried.

This happened to Moses as well. Here was a guy who was born at a time when the pharaoh wanted him dead—along with every other Hebrew baby boy. He was providentially protected by his shrewd mother, who set him afloat in a basket among the reeds on the banks of the Nile, where he would be discovered by the pharaoh's daughter—who better to protect him?—and raised in luxury while his own people endured slavery. As a young man—forty is the new twenty, right?—he failed miserably in his attempt to ease his people's burden. He then had to flee Egypt for fear that his actions might catch up with him.[10]

After decades spent looking over his shoulder as a fugitive on the run, he eventually accepted his new reality and settled into a daily routine. Then one day he spotted a burning bush. Because he lived in the desert, he was probably accustomed to seeing bushes catch fire. But this one kept burning without being destroyed. And if that weren't enough, God started talking to him from it!

God told Moses to go back to the place he'd run away from and to confront the most powerful man in the world with the news that he was about to lose most of his labor force.

God revealed himself, but it wasn't all neat and tidy.

Throughout the Old Testament, God shows up in some interesting ways—in a den of lions, through victories on a battlefield, through the words of prophets, through commands inscribed on stone tablets, and even through a widow's never-ending supply of oil.

We see those examples and think, *Great . . . but I'm not Moses. I'm not Abraham. I'm not David or Elijah. How am I supposed to see God?* I think these stories have been preserved not to suggest that such circumstances are the norm but rather to show us the nature of God. He is a God who wants to reveal himself to us.

That's the truth that Jesus conveys when he says, "Anyone who has seen me has seen the Father." And that's what the apostle Paul says in describing Jesus: "Christ is the visible image of the invisible God."[11]

Here's the good news: God has revealed himself.

For ever since the world was created, people have
seen the earth and sky. Through everything God
made, they can clearly see his invisible qualities—his
eternal power and divine nature. So they have no
excuse for not knowing God.[12]

Here's the bad news: We fail to notice. Here we are, living in God's art gallery, and yet we pay no attention to the artist. As Paul has said, there's really no excuse.

David reminds us that creation is always revealing its Creator.

The heavens declare the glory of God;
    the skies proclaim the work of his hands.
Day after day they pour forth speech;
    night after night they reveal knowledge.
They have no speech, they use no words;
    no sound is heard from them.
Yet their voice goes out into all the earth,
    their words to the ends of the world.[13]

Yes, even before the Bible was written, people had the ability to know God. Even before the coming of Jesus, people had the ability to see God. Before the patriarchs, the disciples, and the desert fathers . . . people could know God. Before churches and podcasts and contemporary Christian music and books like this one . . . they could know God. Before WWJD bracelets and dashboard saints and Testamints . . . they could know God. (If you don't know what Testamints are . . . well, you're better off not knowing.)

But they stopped knowing him when they stopped doing two things: *worshiping* and *giving thanks.* "Yes, they knew God," Paul writes, "but they wouldn't worship him as God or even give him thanks."[14] Simply put, they stopped noticing God and stopped saying "thank you."

> They began to think up foolish ideas of what God was like. As a result, their minds became dark and confused. Claiming to be wise, they instead became utter fools. And instead of worshiping the glorious, ever-living God, they worshiped idols made to look like mere people and birds and animals and reptiles.[15]

The ramifications were huge. When people stopped noticing God and stopped thanking him for all he had done, something snapped. In the absence of reverence, people came up with new theories about God that they thought were brilliant but were actually foolish. As a result, they became even more confused—to the point that they started worshiping animals.

It's hard to imagine that just failing to notice the Creator would turn into worshiping the creation. But we fall prey to this all the time. It happens when we decide that we don't really want God—we just want his stuff.

Go with me on this for just a moment. Imagine that, for some odd reason, we became confused about night and day—to the point that we began to see the moon as our primary source of light and heat. Everyone would put on moonscreen and moonglasses and go outside to work on their moontan. It would change some of our music. George Harrison would have sung, "Here comes the moon." Sheryl Crow would have sung, "I'm gonna soak up the moon." And the Brady Bunch would have entered that talent show to sing, "It's a moon-shine day." We'd bring our tomato plants out during the night but bring them in during the day. This is ridiculous, of course, because we know that the moon isn't a heat source or even a reliable light source. The moon simply reflects the sun.

Noticing God Again

When we struggle with our belief in God, it's often because we've become too focused on the creation rather than the Creator. When we struggle with disappointment, frustration, and anger, it's because we've asked our spouse to be something that only God can be, or we've asked our job to provide something that only God can supply, or we've demanded that our kids give us the kind of significance that only God can impart. In short, we've asked the moon to do something that only the sun can do.

But what if we returned to noticing God and saying thank you? According to David, we will increase in wisdom, joy, insight, purity, truth, and justice.

> The instructions of the LORD are perfect,
>> reviving the soul.
> The decrees of the LORD are trustworthy,
>> making wise the simple.
> The commandments of the LORD are right,
>> bringing joy to the heart.
> The commands of the LORD are clear,
>> giving insight for living.
> Reverence for the LORD is pure,
>> lasting forever.
> The laws of the LORD are true;
>> each one is fair.
> They are more desirable than gold,
>> even the finest gold.
> They are sweeter than honey,
>> even honey dripping from the comb.[16]

There are four primary avenues by which we notice God: *Scripture, creation, people,* and *circumstances.*

- *Scripture.* Not only was the Bible God's Word to its original hearers; it is God's Word to us as well. Jesus followers down through the ages have agreed that the primary way God communicates and reveals himself is through Scripture. Simple fact: People who regularly read the Bible hear God speak more often than those who don't. When we read God's Word, he partners with us to communicate to us.

- *Creation.* This is what David speaks of in Psalms 19 and 65. He looked at the vastness of creation—sun, moon, stars, mountains, oceans, etc.—and heard nonverbal whispers from God about God's power, care, and attention. In noticing God's creation, we partner with him in appreciating his handiwork.

- *People.* God often speaks to us through other people— a pastor delivering a message, a parent reassuring us of love, a friend encouraging us to grow, or even an enemy criticizing our blind spots. I once heard author Bob Goff say, "The reason God doesn't speak to me audibly is because then I'd stop listening to *you!*" In paying attention to others, we partner with God in order to hear him.

- *Circumstances.* God is quite capable of communicating through the details of your life. Not everything that happens is God speaking, which is why God often combines this form of communication with another;

but through our circumstances, God partners with us to converse with us.

In all of these situations, take time to notice God and say, "Thank you."

On your way to work, notice what God has made and say, "Thank you." When having lunch with friends or coworkers, notice how God has made us all unique and yet interdependent and say, "Thank you." When spending time with your family over a meal, notice the joy that laughter brings and say, "Thank you." When reading through the Gospels, notice how Jesus loves the unlovely, heals the broken, and saves the sinner. Then recognize that he's done the same thing for you and say, "Thank you."

Our noisy, hectic, busy lives remind me of the story of Elijah. He experienced all the signs and wonders you'd think God would use to communicate—a mighty rushing wind, an earthquake, and even a fire, but the Lord's voice was not heard in any of them. Instead, God spoke to Elijah in a still, small whisper after all the flash and fury were gone.[17] Sometimes we have to get quiet enough to hear his voice. He doesn't tend to shout over the noise in our lives.

> When we quiet our hearts and take time to notice God, then we'll see that he's always here.

When we quiet our hearts and take time to notice God, then we'll see that he's always here.

when you

INVEST

in God's

KINGDOM,

then

GOD

will

INVEST

in

YOURS

Our family loves going to the beach. Because we live only an hour away, you'd think we would go more often, but it's not as often as you'd expect. For one thing, California beaches are not quite as inviting as they appear on TV. Because of issues related to simple longitude and latitude, they tend to be not quite as warm as you might think. The water temperature is usually a very uncomfortable 55 degrees. There have been many times when, while packing up the minivan to head to the beach, we tossed in the coats and blankets as well.

Because actually going into the water can be less than pleasant, we find other things to do when we're at the beach. We take the kids on long walks along the shore while I playfully irritate everyone by kicking the cold water onto their legs. Sometimes we'll take a bucket along and the girls will look for shells. Occasionally, we'll even bring our two dogs. (But even though the dogs love it, we don't like having to bathe them when we get home.)

My favorite thing to do at the beach is to sit in a chair and watch the waves roll in. Something about the endless surge of the ocean and the limitless horizon puts my world into perspective. The only problem is that sitting and relaxing doesn't make the cut on my daughters' list of their favorite things. So the only real chance I get to relax and reflect is when they are busy making sand castles. I try to encourage this endeavor by packing and schlepping all the buckets, shovels, and rakes they'll need to facilitate their construction projects. Once the girls are busy, my wife and I will set up our chairs (and an umbrella, if needed), position the cooler for maximum convenience, and settle in to enjoy the rhythm of the sea. Occasionally, I'll make a helpful suggestion to keep the girls' process going—"You should add a waterslide" or "Try adding a second story"—but mostly I just sit and stare at the ocean.

Once in a while, each girl will decide to build her own castle. I don't recommend this because it often leads to turf wars. I prefer for them to work together, as we all learned on *Sesame Street*. But you can't stop the entrepreneurial itch, nor can you reason with an opinionated tween. So the independent projects begin—with visions of multiple levels and wings, colonnades, moats, and drawbridges. They use terms such as "an open concept" and "a well-laid-out space." (Clearly we watch too much HGTV!) And after about twenty minutes, the ventures always end the same way—with arguments.

"It's my turn with the bucket!"

"You're building yours too close to mine!"

"Stay away from me!"

"Stop copying me!"

"Daaaaad, she knocked down my castle!"

When you're building a kingdom, all you care about is your own castle.

Our kingdoms may not contain sand castles, but we all have something we're building and trying to maintain.

For many of us, our kingdom includes our families—our spouse, some kids, aging parents, siblings, cousins, nieces and nephews, aunts, and the crazy uncle we never speak of.

Our families may even include our friends. I don't mean the hundreds—or thousands—of Facebook friends you have; I mean those you would actually want to have coffee with. Perhaps a few neighbors, some friends from work, your Bible study group at church, and a couple of the parents at your kids' school.

Pastor Larry Osborne says that people are like Legos. We all have a need for connection, but we have a finite amount of space for it. Some of us are two-stud Legos; others are like the big green sheets with hundreds of studs. No matter how big your Lego piece is, that's your family. And for many of us, it's the kingdom we protect.

Our kingdom might also contain our work. It might be a career that we've worked hard to build. It might be a small business that we started with borrowed money and rented facilities but now have built into something substantial. It might just be a job. We don't love it, but it pays the bills. We need it, so we get up and go every day. This is the kingdom others of us choose to protect.

For many of us, our kingdom is our own person. We exercise, read, meditate, rest, or eat things that some would call lawn clippings but that we call *lunch*. We study about clean and healthy living, we focus on our weight and cholesterol, and we do our best to get the amount of sleep we need. We go to great lengths to protect this kingdom.

Also for many of us, our kingdom is our estate. We don't use that word, but this "estate" involves all our wealth—our houses, cars, stocks, investments, insurance, and retirement.

We've managed our money well, but it's been a lot of work. We read about it, study the market trends, and have our financial advisors on speed dial—all because this is the kingdom we protect.

Most of us can relate to all of these things. Our kingdom portfolios include a variety of interests and investments—personal, monetary, and relational. It's the kingdom of Me. And each of us works hard to build it and protect it.

We each worry about our own kingdom. How long will it last? Do I have enough resources to build it? What if someone tries to take it from me?

We compare our kingdoms. What do others think of me? Am I valued? Do they look down on me?

We fight for our kingdoms. We lie to get more. We steal to provide. We attack others who seem to be a threat.

Am I sinning by caring about my own kingdom? Can I even ask God to care about my kingdom?

But how does all this stack up against Matthew 6:33: "Seek the Kingdom of God above all else, and live righteously"?

I guess the bigger questions are these: *Am I even allowed to have a kingdom? Am I sinning by caring about my own kingdom? Can I even ask God to care about my kingdom?*

This is where I struggle with my kingdom. I feel tremendous pressure that I'm in this all by myself. I've felt this way about leading our church. When our church was young, small, and taking on the big project of buying land and constructing a building, I faced many sleepless nights.

"How are we going to afford this?"

"What if no one shows up?"

I know that the movie *Field of Dreams* says, "If you build it, they will come," but I was thinking, "If we build it, they *better* come!" We had climbed way out on the limb of faith, and it seemed as if the branch was starting to crack. I know it's not *my* church. I know it belongs to God. But I'm the caretaker, so I worry about it. And I'm embarrassed to admit how many times I've thought of it as *my* kingdom.

Think about the theories we've heard all our lives that we assume are godly:

"God helps those who help themselves." This is probably one of the most often quoted Bible verses that is not actually in the Bible. It is frequently attributed to Ben Franklin's *Poor Richard's Almanack*.

"If it's meant to be, it's up to me." This belief puts more pressure on us and completely ignores God. After all, if he doesn't care about anything in my kingdom, it all falls on me.

"Pray as if it all depends on God. Work as if it all depends on me." Though this sounds like one of our When/Then equations, it can actually do more harm than good. It lures us into thinking that God isn't all that interested in helping us—we'll ask anyway, but we just shouldn't expect much.

These quotations aren't in the Bible, but we act as if they were!

Some of us prefer to put all the responsibility for kingdom management onto God. The moment anything goes wrong with our kingdoms, we assume that it's by God's neglect and that it's now God's responsibility to fix it. Think about our prayers and how they often focus on one of three things: *help me, bless me,* or *protect me.* These are all personal-kingdom management prayers. And none has anything to do with our participation in God's Kingdom.

The mother of James and John had personal-kingdom priorities on her mind when she approached Jesus and said, "In your Kingdom, please let my two sons sit in places of honor next to you, one on your right and the other on your left."[1] It might appear that she was asking about Jesus' Kingdom, but her motive was to promote her own family's kingdom. She was fine with Jesus being the CEO, just as long as her boys got to be the CFO and COO.

> Think about our prayers and how they often focus on one of three things: *help me, bless me,* or *protect me.*

Jesus' response reveals the nature of his Kingdom: "You don't know what you are asking! . . . My Father has prepared those places for the ones he has chosen."[2] Apparently, advancing our kingdoms at the expense of God's is not possible.

But what if it were possible for us to do *both*?

Our Kingdom Is Provided from His

The first thing we need to see is that everything we have comes from God, as Jesus tells us in the parable of the talents (see Matthew 25:14-30). Our lives, our abilities, our homes, our careers, our families—everything is on loan from God. And it's up to us to manage it well.

In his grace, God has allowed us to enjoy our stewardship of the many things he's placed in our hands. He's allowed us to thrive at work, provide for our families, and create comfortable living spaces. He's allowed us to enjoy the fruits of our labor. And when we manage his things well, he often entrusts us with more. The "talents" belong to God, but we are able to enjoy them as we invest them and put them to use.

Occasionally, my youngest daughter forgets whose house she's living in. She'll draw up blueprints and make plans for some renovations and color changes in her bedroom that not only are costly but also will require a lot of my assistance.

When I balk at the proposed changes, she'll often say, "But it's *my* room!"

My response at this point is to remind her that she didn't buy the house, and she's never paid a nickel on the mortgage, and thus it really isn't her room. Truth be told, the entire house belongs to the bank for the next twenty years or so.

But lately, she has discovered that when she takes care of the responsibilities she's been given, I'm more likely to invest in and help her decorate her room.

Though most of us are nervous and hesitant about asking God to bless not only his own Kingdom but also ours, God doesn't shy away from talking about it. We feel as if it's a sacrilege to even consider our own kingdoms. Shouldn't we consider only God's Kingdom and sacrifice everything for him? Most of us spend our lives secretly trying to manage our own kingdoms while feeling convicted that we should give them up for God. Isn't that what "turn from your selfish ways, take up your cross daily, and follow me" is all about?[3] But God knows we have things to manage, build, invest in, create, and lead. After all, he's the one who gave us those people, ideas, talents, and wealth to lead, manage, and develop. He's the one who allowed us to have that small kingdom in the first place. The real question is this: How do our kingdoms advance his Kingdom? As long as our kingdoms aren't working in opposition to his, he wants to partner with us in advancing both.

> As long as our kingdoms aren't working in opposition to his, he wants to partner with us in advancing both.

Still not convinced? Let's take a closer look at the partnership God offers us.

In 2 Corinthians, Paul writes to a group of people who were living in a much worse economy than we have now. They were paying about 40 percent of their income in taxes. They had no 401(k) and no health insurance; they didn't even have the lottery! Nevertheless, Paul writes, "Remember this: Whoever sows sparingly will also reap sparingly, and whoever sows generously will also reap generously."[4]

He doesn't say, "Just sow and be happy with whatever you get" or "Sow and expect nothing from God." Instead, he says, "Sow generously and expect a big harvest!" The measure by which you sow is the measure by which you will reap.

We see this principle play out in every area of our lives.

Think about your marriage. If you spend quality time with your spouse, take vacations, keep his or her needs ahead of your own, and grow together spiritually, you will reap a loving marriage that will last.

Think about this with your career. If you sow into your job by working hard, meeting your goals, presenting a great attitude, and being coachable, you will reap a successful career.

Think about this with all of life. When you sow generously into God's Kingdom, then he takes a vested interest in yours.

God Asks Us to Invest in His Kingdom

When you read the Gospels, you see that the quality of people's lives goes up when Jesus comes around. The blind can see, the lame can walk, and the sick are healed. God's Kingdom is one in which people are made whole not only spiritually but also physically, emotionally, and mentally. God wants us to sow generously into the quality of people's lives.

We see this in an encounter between Jesus and a certain wealthy young landholder. This young man is a successful real-estate entrepreneur and has amassed many properties. But he is not just a businessman. He is, as we might say, in touch with his spiritual side. He has a deep yearning for God, and he seeks out Jesus in order to ask him how to attain everlasting life. Jesus replies that it is simple: Follow God's commands. After Jesus lists a few examples, the young man proudly declares, "All these I have kept since I was a boy." Then Jesus looks at him and says, "Go, sell everything you have and give to the poor, and you will have treasure in heaven. Then come, follow me."[5]

God doesn't hesitate to ask us for money, because it's all his in the first place. There are no self-generated assets because God has made everything that exists. To say nothing of the fact that God made you; therefore, by builders' rights, you and everything you own belong to him.

God Gladly Invests in Our Kingdoms

God doesn't just say, "Okay, give me back all your money because it was mine in the first place" and walk off gruffly, having muscled us into doing our religious duty. Instead, he promises his involvement in our lives. In the case of the wealthy young landholder, it is a promise to be involved in his future Kingdom and his current peace of mind. When we invest in what God is interested in, he'll invest in what interests us.

This partnership is what Paul emphasizes in 2 Corinthians 9. Sow generously into the things that God is interested in. Invest your life, your talent, your time, and especially your treasure into the advancement of God's Kingdom, and God will sow generously into the things you're interested in. He will invest in your kingdom. This promise is what frees us from worry about our own kingdom.

Maybe that still seems hard to accept. Why would God do that? Is it even true? Isn't that "prosperity gospel" teaching?

Let's look at a time when God's people made the decision to stop sowing generously—a time when they started using all their resources for themselves and giving only the leftovers to God. Not only did God stop blessing them generously, but he also got pretty offended by their actions. Yet when he confronted them, he offered the same When/Then promise.

In 400 BC, near the end of the time recorded in the Old Testament, God's people invested in his Kingdom by bringing him animal sacrifices. It would have been easy for the people to offer only their scrawny or sickly lambs that wouldn't yield much wealth, but God asked for the best of the best—only pure and spotless lambs. When God's people began to compromise their standards, God sent a prophet named Malachi to speak on his behalf.

> Will a mere mortal rob God? Yet you rob me.
> But you ask, "How are we robbing you?"
> In tithes and offerings. You are under a curse—
> your whole nation—because you are robbing me.[6]

If you've ever been robbed, you know it can be a devastating experience. And that's the language that God uses: *I've been robbed . . . and you did it.*

Several years ago at one of our Easter services, we had a strange occurrence. During the offering time, we passed the offering bags as usual; but somewhere in one of the rows, one of the bags disappeared. Granted, the room was crowded and dimly lit, and each usher was managing multiple bags. The usher in that particular section thought, *Maybe the bag was passed forward a row instead of back, and I'm mistaken.* But he wasn't. Between services, we found the missing bag—empty—in the grass outside the building.

I think we'd all agree that it's bad enough to rob someone. It's even worse to rob God. But it's a triple whammy to rob God on Easter! Yet every time we choose not to bring our tithes and offerings to God, says Malachi, we rob him of what is rightfully his.

> Every time we choose not to bring our tithes and offerings to God, we rob him of what is rightfully his.

The word *tithe* simply means a tenth of our income—10 percent. If ever there was a command in the Bible that we tend to view as a Never Mind in our day and age, this would be it. The most common argument against the tithe is that it's outdated—that it's an Old Testament-only thing. After all, Jesus never mentioned the tithe, right? Actually, Jesus refers to tithing several times—not as a new teaching or even as a reinforcement of an old teaching, but in such a way that he assumes we all know about it.

On one occasion, some people ask Jesus whether they should pay taxes. He responds, "Give to Caesar what belongs to Caesar, and give to God what belongs to God."[7] In other words, we should be as faithful in giving our tithes as we are in paying our taxes.

Another time, Jesus challenges the religious leaders of the day for their lack of justice and mercy.

Woe to you, teachers of the law and Pharisees, you hypocrites! You give a tenth of your spices—mint, dill and cumin. But you have neglected the more important matters of the law—justice, mercy and faithfulness. You should have practiced the latter, without neglecting the former.[8]

If Jesus wanted to negate the tithe, wouldn't he do it here? Instead, he says we should both live justly, mercifully, and faithfully *and* tithe—not just one or the other.

The apostle Paul also assumed that people would contribute monetarily to the work of the church. He tells the Corinthians to come on Sunday prepared to give.[9] And he tells Timothy to encourage the church not to put their hope in wealth but to be prepared to give whenever they see a need.[10]

Though the tithe is something that God has determined, we're also called to be generous in giving offerings over and above the tithe. We may give to a special project or event, or give extra just because we want to keep sowing generously.[11]

Here is what Malachi tells us to do not only to make this right but also to partner with God: "Bring the whole tithe into the storehouse, that there may be food in my house."[12]

What is "the storehouse"? In the Old Testament, it was the Temple. In the New Testament and beyond, it is the church. God says that we're to bring our tithes to the local church. The issue is not between you and your pastor. The issue is between you and God.

This is how we invest in his Kingdom.

This is clearly not a Never Mind command. Rather, it's an exciting opportunity to partner with God. In fact, this is one of the most obvious and beneficial When/Thens in the Bible. I have never met anyone who regretted making the decision to give to God. But I have met plenty who regretted not giving. And there's a reason why. Look at what Malachi says God will do if we give:

> "Test me in this," says the LORD Almighty, "and see
> if I will not throw open the floodgates of heaven
> and pour out so much blessing that there will not
> be room enough to store it. I will prevent pests from
> devouring your crops, and the vines in your fields will
> not drop their fruit before it is ripe," says the LORD
> Almighty.[13]

I find this fascinating. Just one verse earlier, we read of God's anger about being robbed by us. If you've ever been robbed and you find out who did it, you want justice! You want everything back—with interest! You want the thieves prosecuted to the full extent of the law. You don't offer them a partnership. But God says, "Bring back what you took! And not only will I forgive you; I will *bless* you!" If we will invest in his Kingdom, he'll invest in ours in such a way that we won't know what to do with all the blessings.

He even says, "Test me."

This is the only place in the Bible where God invites us

to test him. And it all comes back to the principle of sowing and reaping. If we make the decision to sow generously, we will reap generously.

This is how God invests in our kingdom when we invest in his.

So how does it work? If I give 10 percent, will God give me 30 percent? Perhaps 40 percent? How much? What can I count on so I can put it in the budget?

It's important to understand that God diversifies his portfolio when he invests in our kingdom.

Sometimes (but not always) the investment is financial

When I teach these principles at our church, I can pretty much mark my calendar three months out for when I'll start receiving e-mails from people telling me their tithing stories.

One couple in our church said they were convicted about tithing, so they sat down one night and adjusted their budget to free up 10 percent for giving. This was a real stretch for them, but they agreed that they needed to do it. On Tuesday of that week, while the husband was away on a business trip, the wife wrote a check for their tithe and mailed it in. She thought, *If this is what God wants, why wait until Sunday?*

When the husband returned home on Friday, they were catching up about their week when he said, "Oh, I forgot to tell you, I got a promotion and a raise."

"When did that happen?" his wife asked.

"Tuesday."

Another woman in our church stopped me one day and said, "I have to tell you my tithing story."

"Let's hear it!" I said.

She went on to tell me how, for years, she had managed her family's books and had multiple credit cards she kept hidden from her husband. He thought they were out of debt and fully tithing, but she knew that wasn't true. Finally, when she had maxed out multiple cards and created a financial predicament she couldn't get out of, she decided to come clean.

Her husband's response was brilliant. With love and grace he said, "We'll get out of this together . . . and with God's help."

They set up a plan not only to start tithing but also to pay the tithe they had neglected over the past few years. This woman looked at me with tears in her eyes and said, "I don't know how God did it . . . but not only were we able to pay back the tithe, but we also got out of debt in record time!"

I do believe the fastest way to get out of debt is to get right with God financially.

I even have a friend who was a skeptic in his belief about God. When he heard us talk about tithing one Sunday, he told his wife, "I don't believe it, so I'm going to try it just to prove it wrong." They gave a gift on Sunday, and on Monday when he got to work, he had an e-mail from human resources requesting to see him. He went in, and they said, "We were looking at your vacation time last year, and it looks as if we owe you some money for the days you didn't use. Here's a check." You guessed it—it was for the exact amount he had given on Sunday. Sometimes giving is the best way to begin to believe in God.

I almost hesitate to share some of those stories because half the people who hear them think it's a version of "prosperity gospel," and the other half wonder why it hasn't worked for them. I had a woman come up to me in our coffeehouse one day and ask, "I hear

> I believe the fastest way to get out of debt is to get right with God financially.

you mention God's blessings in my life . . . but when can I expect that to happen?" She wanted to know when the check would arrive in her mailbox as it seemed to have done for everyone else. Did God not have her address? But God diversifies his investments. And his blessings are never limited to the realm of finances.

Sometimes the blessing is business

I had lunch with a small-business owner in our church during the height of the Great Recession. I asked him how the economy was affecting his business, and he said that it had been tough until a few months ago. I asked him what had happened a few months ago and he said, "That's when I decided to start tithing. Since then, the phone won't stop ringing. I've got more business than I've ever had!"

One Sunday, a man came up to me and shared his giving story. He said that he'd been out of work for two years but that he and his wife had decided to find a way to sow generously for God. They pooled together all the money they had left to see if they could make it till the end of the year. Then they tithed from what they had. Two days later, he got a job.

Sometimes the blessing is longevity

I've seen this one in my own life. For years, my wife and I drove two cars that just would not die. This was a blessing because they were paid off, but they were still old. Sure, we had a trusted mechanic who kept them together, but there was only so much he could do. God apparently did the rest. Many times I wished he would stop "blessing" them so much, but he helped them last a lot longer than they should have. Sometimes, God allows a car, a washer or dryer, or a roof over our heads to last longer than it should. Sometimes, he even does this with our health!

Sometimes the blessing is protection

Even though you may face financial storms, there's tremendous blessing in knowing that you have an umbrella of protection in God. I've never met anyone who said, "I've saved up enough from not tithing so that I don't need God's help with my life and my finances." We all want God to be involved in our lives. When we invest in his Kingdom, he stays involved with ours.

A woman named Jenny taught me this. For years, she had led her family to church and had set the pace with tithing, even though her husband, who was an alcoholic, barely provided for the family's needs. Jenny had repeatedly appealed to his better nature, asking that he get help—not only for the sake of their marriage but also for the well-being of their young daughter. She volunteered to join him at recovery meetings and tried to get him to go to counseling. He'd show up a few times and then quit.

After a few years of this, she finally asked him to move out and served him with divorce papers—to protect both herself and her daughter. By then he had lost his job and was no longer providing anything for the family, and he was slipping even deeper into his abuse of alcohol.

> Though you may face financial storms, there's tremendous blessing in knowing that you have an umbrella of protection in God.

I'll never forget the day Jenny called to update me on her situation: Her husband was now demanding alimony from her. Yes, an out-of-work, alcoholic husband was demanding beer money from the soon-to-be-single mother of his child. Or that's how it looked to me.

I was expecting her to be angry with God, wondering where her blessings were and assuming that God had abandoned her. Instead, she told a story of God's protection. Even though her income had taken a significant hit, God was faithful by helping her make ends meet. And even when she, too, lost her job, God provided a better one. Her faith never wavered during this time because she knew that God would provide. And that's what God did. Though she walked through a raging storm, God walked alongside her, holding the umbrella.

Sometimes the blessing is contentment

Just knowing that God is at work in our world and interested in our interests is far more comforting than relying on a volatile stock market for our future provision. The apostle Paul said that he had learned to be content in all circumstances, and we can learn that contentment as well.[14]

> The apostle Paul said that he had learned to be content in all circumstances, and we can learn that contentment as well.

I've learned in my own life that, if scarcity is a cancer that eats away at our contentment, generosity is the cure. Recently, our family took a trip to the Universal Studios theme park in Orlando. As much as I love to see my kids have a great time, and as much as I enjoy the rides, there are three things that can ruin my day: heat, crowds, and overpriced food. This trip was guaranteed to have all three—at record highs!

After we'd been at the park for about an hour, we were already exhausted and soaked with sweat, and I had nearly come to blows with a few people in line. The place was packed. So we decided to cool off over lunch at a little café. When I saw the prices, it didn't help my blood pressure.

I was trying my best to put on a happy face for my kids when I heard my wife say, "Let's pay for another table along with ours."

I said, "That's great!" but my eyes said, "Are you kidding me?" to my wife.

My kids loved the idea. (Of course they did; they weren't paying!) But I agreed. I tried to suggest a table with only one person, but the others settled on a nearby table with a young family. When the server came by, I asked for our check and theirs. The server was shocked and then quite moved by the gesture.

My daughters were giddy with excitement at this sneaky mission we had embarked upon. We watched out of the corners of our eyes while the server told the family that their check had been covered. They looked stunned.

I don't know exactly how what we did affected that family—though the server told us later that the mom began to tear up—but I know how it affected my family. The rest of our day became one of "whom can we bless next?" My daughters bought water for people, we let people go ahead of us in line—and, to my surprise, I relaxed. I saw the crowds as a mission field. I saw our money as something we could use to help other people. And I even forgot about the heat (though maybe not the humidity). In a word, we were *content*. And *generosity* is what brought that blessing to our day.

Sometimes the greatest blessing we receive is knowing that we are making an eternal impact

One of the reasons that many people save and hoard money is the hope that they will somehow both meet their own needs and also leave a legacy, either by leaving the money for their kids or by bequeathing a generous gift to a charitable organization. But when we bring our tithes to the local church, we are able to pool our money together with others' to make an eternal impact in people's lives.

As much as I love and support the many organizations that are working to end disease, we all will die from something even if they succeed, and we'll be faced with an eternity somewhere. When I invest in God's Kingdom, sometimes the greatest gift I receive is the joy of seeing baptisms and dedications and people choosing to follow Jesus. That's the mission of the local church I'm invested in.

Here's something I have noticed without exception: Every tither I have ever met says, "God has blessed me so much." And every non-tither I have ever met says, "I can't afford to tithe."

Think about that for a moment.

If you're not tithing now and you begin to tithe, you may very well experience financial or material blessings. I know countless people and families who have made the difficult decision to start tithing or giving over and above the norm. And though it may have taken them a while to get used to parting with their capital, before too long they have begun to marvel regularly at how God has taken care of their material needs. I have yet to meet someone—not even one—who started giving regularly and later regretted it.

Why would we want to stop partnering with God in the work of Kingdom investment? When we advance his Kingdom, we worry less about our own, and he gives us far more than we could ever imagine or deserve.

Test him in this. He invites you.

chapter eight

When you show KINDNESS to others, then God will show them GRACE

In the heart of Los Angeles is a movie theater that was made for the true movie enthusiast. The ArcLight Cinema chain has multiple locations, but it's the one in Hollywood that is extra special. As you approach, you know something magical is happening. From the street you can see the searchlights directing you to the theater. When you walk in, there are movie costumes, props, and even cars displayed along the sidewalk to celebrate the latest film release. As you approach the concession stand, you smell something that has become endangered—popcorn with real movie-theater butter. If you ask, they will *layer* it for you. This technique was taught to me by the fine people who work there. They start with a layer of popcorn, then a layer of butter, then another layer of popcorn, then another layer of butter. You're on your own for the salt, but they've got the butter.

Though the building has fourteen screens for multiple movies, the Cinerama Dome is its crown jewel. The Cinerama is literally a dome, with an eighty-six-foot screen paired with the best sound system available. It creates an experience not to be forgotten. But as great as the building, the props, the popcorn, and the Cinerama Dome are, they are not everything that makes the ArcLight the greatest theater in the world. No, on top of all those world-class features, the ArcLight also offers *reserved seats*. No more waiting in long lines, fighting the crowds, and braving the stampede to avoid getting stuck in the front row. The ArcLight allows you to predetermine your seat when you purchase your tickets online. Now you may enter like a civilized person, without having to worry about spilling your two thousand calories of popcorn. This is a great house for the art and science of motion pictures.

For me, going to the ArcLight is what going to Disneyland is to the rest of my family. They are experiences to be treasured but not overdone. Even though we can easily drive to both places, we really shouldn't go all the time. We don't want to end up taking it all for granted. So my friends and I plan strategic trips to the ArcLight based on the release of huge blockbuster films that are worthy of the Dome. I say "my friends and I" because my wife and kids couldn't care less. They'd be fine at the local theater. I, on the other hand, prefer not to be stuck behind a bunch of teens texting throughout an uplifting spiritual experience like *The Avengers*.

> When we have a transcendent experience, we want to share it—with everyone.

Speaking of great movies, when the final Batman movie was coming out several years ago, I knew it would require a trip to the ArcLight. I'm a bit of a fan, and I knew that *The Dark Knight Rises* would be a great finale to the trilogy. So I booked tickets for myself and a few friends. I was so excited about the movie that I couldn't wait until the week—or even the day—after its release to see it. We had to get tickets for the very first showing of the film—at midnight!

My friends and I drove down early to Sunset Boulevard,

had some dinner and a lot of coffee, and headed to the theater. The place was buzzing with excitement when we arrived. Superfans were strolling around with their own costumes, the lights were chasing each other about, and the popcorn called to me from the parking lot. You can keep Mickey. This was *my* Disneyland!

The movie lived up to the hype. I loved every minute of it. Despite my age and the fact that it was way past my bedtime, I was energized during the entire two hours and forty-five minutes of the movie and during the drive home. It was so good that I began texting people on the way home, telling them, "You've got to go see this." (If I woke them up, it was their own fault for not using their phone's do-not-disturb feature.) Instead of trying to be as quiet as possible when I arrived home at 3:30 a.m., I might have shut the door a little hard. Maybe I clicked on a light in our bedroom when I could have used my phone light. When Lorrie woke up, I played dumb and apologized, but truth be told I was hoping she would wake up. I couldn't wait to tell her all about the movie. And I actually wanted her to go with me to see it again—right then. (I believe there was another showing at 5:00 a.m.) She politely declined, or maybe she just went back to sleep and forgot the entire conversation. But I didn't sleep a wink. I just kept texting people.

We've all had an experience like that. It might not have been a great movie at a great theater. It might have been an exquisite meal at a great restaurant or a fantastic vacation at an exotic destination. But when we have a transcendent experience, we want to share it with everyone. We want all our friends and family to have the same experience we've had. We text, tweet, Instagram, and share all our pictures and recommendations. And we'll stop at nothing to get everyone else to discover what we've found.

So why is it that we can easily share information about movies, theaters, restaurants, a sale at the Gap, or a time-share in Cabo, but when it comes to our relationship with Jesus . . . we just keep it to ourselves? Many of us have had the experience of beginning our faith journey, growing in our relationship with Jesus, and having him transform our lives. Then we think of all the people who we wish could find what we've found. But often we hesitate or simply keep our mouths shut. We justify it by telling ourselves, "Oh, they wouldn't understand" or "I wouldn't want to offend them" or "It's a personal thing."

It's not for a lack of satisfaction. We are overwhelmed by the grace of God expressed through the death of Jesus on the cross. We relish the forgiveness of sin and the freedom from shame we now have. We look forward to eternity in heaven and live each day with that hope in mind. Who wouldn't want to share that? That's a lot better than movie-theater popcorn!

What tends to button our lips is the fear of how we will be perceived. We don't want to be like that crazy guy on the street corner with the bullhorn, or the religious zealot at the office whom everyone avoids like the plague. Or maybe it's that we don't want to be seen as hypocrites. After all, we're not perfect: We each have our own past, and to suddenly start talking about Jesus may come off as a bit insincere. For many of us, we don't want to venture into a conversation that might lead to questions we can't answer. We don't feel as if we know enough or are good enough, so we just keep quiet.

Those of us who live with a high sense of guilt, whose faith is anchored in the Thou Shalts, think the responsibility for saving everyone rests squarely on our shoulders. When I was in high school, part of our church's youth ministry included "Tuesday night calling." We'd load up a car with a few other students and go visit someone at his or her home who had attended our church the week before. Our goal was to thank these people for coming, invite them to return, and ask them about their faith in Jesus. If they were new to the whole thing, our hope and prayer was to lead them to faith in Jesus through a progression we referred to as the Five Finger Exercise: *hear, believe, confess, repent,* and *be baptized.* The preferred place for all this was in their living rooms, but we could pull it off on the front porch through the screen door, if necessary. There was nothing like the feeling of utter rejection and failure as we left house after house. But we'd come back and do it again the next week because we felt that the eternal destiny of all these people was in our hands, as if their salvation were our responsibility.

Though door-to-door calling is not quite as common today, we use other methods when we feel as if the responsibility is all ours. There are the salvation pleas we post on Facebook: "Like this post if you're ready to receive Jesus." There are leaflets we can leave on car windshields and restaurant tables that are designed to lead someone to Christ even without our having to be there. And there is the more personal approach of simply heaping guilt on someone who seems resistant.

"Why don't you come to church with me . . . you'll make God happy!"

"Do you know that that language makes God cry?"

"Do you like heat? Well, you'd better get used to it!"

Obviously I'm exaggerating (a bit), but many of us are overwhelmed with guilt because we don't have much success with sharing our faith, and thus we rarely do it. This doesn't seem like partnership.

The opposite extreme is to assume that if someone is meant to be saved, God will take care of it. It's up to God to get their attention. He did that for Paul. He did that for the disciples. If God wants someone to accept him, he can certainly create another Damascus Road experience.

This sentiment is often expressed in statements like this: "I'm just hoping to set a good example so they will get the hint." It's as if we believe that if we are really good church people, our pagan neighbors will see us coming home from church one day and will flag us down to say, "Tell me about this Jesus you serve!"

Though it's no doubt true that some people come to Christ all on their own, God seems to want to partner with us in reaching others.

Look at what Paul says about the great gift of salvation we have received:

Christ's love compels us, because we are convinced
that one died for all, and therefore all died. . . .

Therefore, if anyone is in Christ, the new
creation has come: The old has gone, the new is
here! All this is from God, who reconciled us to
himself through Christ and gave us the ministry of
reconciliation: that God was reconciling the world to
himself in Christ, not counting people's sins against
them. And he has committed to us the message of
reconciliation. We are therefore Christ's ambassadors,
as though God were making his appeal through us.[1]

By partnering with God and his plan for our lives, we become
part of his reconciliation-and-renovation project for the
world. God's plan is for people who
are far from him to come near, and
he enlists our help in this endeavor
"to seek and save those who are
lost."[2] God has given us the privilege of partnering with him in
spreading the great news of salvation through the person and work
of Jesus Christ. This great plan has
nothing to do with our perfection or our intellect. Nor does it
have anything to do with grabbing a bullhorn and a sandwich
board and standing on a street corner.

Look how Jesus describes it:

> God has given us the
> privilege of partnering
> with him in spreading the
> great news of salvation
> through Jesus Christ.

You are the light of the world. A town built on a hill cannot be hidden. Neither do people light a lamp and put it under a bowl. Instead they put it on its stand, and it gives light to everyone in the house. In the same way, let your light shine before others, that they may see your good deeds and glorify your Father in heaven.[3]

When we let our light shine, *then* others begin to glorify God. How can that be?

Paul, in his letter to the Romans, tells us something interesting about God's role in this evangelism partnership: "God's kindness is intended to lead you to repentance."[4] In other words, it is not God's intellect, logic, judgment, or condemnation that compels us to follow him, but rather his *kindness*.

This is how Jesus established his Kingdom. In the Gospels, we see how he extends grace to Matthew despite Matthew's occupation as a tax collector. We see how he offers kindness to a woman dragged out into the street to be stoned after being caught in the act of adultery. We see how he made lunch plans with a notorious crook named Zacchaeus and gave him a second chance. And the list goes on. What this tells me is that, if we want to share the grace and truth of Jesus, we must do it in the spirit of Jesus—that is, with kindness, grace, and mercy.

Not only does Jesus *demonstrate* kindness; he also rewards it in others.

In one of the more dramatic episodes recorded of people

trying to get to Jesus, we see four men carry their paralyzed friend on a makeshift gurney to the house where Jesus is teaching. When they find the place so crowded that they can't even get to the front door, much less get a front-row seat for their party of five, they decide to make a hole in the roof and lower him down at the feet of Jesus.[5]

I have to be honest; I'm not sure I would have thought of that! Jesus is teaching to a packed house when, suddenly, chunks of plaster and mud and thatch begin to fall from the ceiling. When everyone looks up, they see a man on a mat being lowered into the presence of Jesus. If this were to happen today, we might assume that it was an object lesson that Jesus had staged as a dramatic conclusion to his message. But this is long before special effects and Cirque du Soleil. These are four loyal friends so desperate to get their buddy to Jesus that they don't allow crowds or roofs or chunks of plaster hitting Jesus on the head to stand in their way.

What happens next is fascinating: "Seeing their faith, Jesus said to the paralyzed man, 'My child, your sins are forgiven.'"[6]

What's stunning about this is that Jesus refers to the *friends'* faith, not the faith of the paralyzed man. There is no great confession, just the kindness and faithfulness of the four men carrying the mat. Their act of kindness garnered forgiveness—and eventually healing—for their ailing friend. Partnering with God involves acts of kindness that bring others to Jesus so that Jesus can extend grace to them.

Years ago, I became convicted that I was not carrying

anyone on a mat to Jesus. I didn't even know anyone who didn't know Jesus. My family, neighbors, and coworkers all were Christians. How could I help someone find the grace of Jesus if everyone I knew already had their reservations in heaven?

I used to think that in order to help people discover what I had found about Jesus, I needed to know the answer to *everything*. I thought I needed to deal with Creation and evolution, explain why bad things happen to good people, and solve theological mysteries such as what happened to the dinosaurs and whether Adam and Eve had belly buttons.

> I used to think that in order to help people discover Jesus, I needed to know the answer to everything.

But here's what the stories of Jesus remind me about: Helping people connect with him begins with my showing kindness. I don't help them by learning how to debate them, by having all the right answers, or by rehearsing a sales pitch to woo them into the Kingdom. Those are the kinds of behavior that lead people to say things such as "I like Jesus, just not his friends."

Having been convicted of a distinct lack of kindness in my life, I decided to put this principle into practice. I decided to start by simply extending kindness to people in my neighborhood and seeing where God took it from there.

Lorrie and I invited people over for dinner; I mowed neighbor's lawns; Lorrie baked cookies; our kids invited other kids over to play; we went to concerts. We even went to watch friends sing at a karaoke bar. Extending kindness to others quickly became one of the greatest joys in my life. What began as a way to share the truth about Jesus quickly became the foundation for a deep community with dear friends. And eventually those friends started taking steps on a spiritual journey of their own.

Not long after this breakthrough discovery, Lorrie and I decided to host a barbecue at our house. I went through the neighborhood putting information about the big event on everyone's door. Then I invited a group of friends from the church to come as well. I figured if we had some critical mass out on the front lawn, others might decide to join us.

When the day came, that was exactly what happened. I wheeled my grill out onto the driveway and started grilling some burgers. My friends from church were shooting hoops and throwing the football around. Gradually, people from the neighborhood began to walk cautiously over to our house. You could see "What's the catch?" written all over their faces. But they ate, talked, and laughed, and my wife and friends and I got to know them.

Out of this simple barbecue grew a friendship with a great couple who lived down the street and had young kids the same ages as ours. In fact, we seemed to have everything in common with Sam and Ellie except one thing: *church*.

Lorrie started walking with Ellie, and our kids started having playdates. When Sam and I discovered that we had a love for movies in common, we would occasionally slip out to see the latest action film after the kids went to bed.

One day, after many months of playdates, movies, and dinners, Ellie asked Lorrie about the church. So Lorrie invited her to come and check it out. Ellie said that it had been years since she'd been to church and that she'd be interested, but she was certain that Sam didn't even believe in God and that he'd probably sit this one out.

Sure enough, the next week, Ellie came to church alone. She sat with Lorrie and seemed to enjoy the service.

Later that night, my kids decided that we needed to start praying for Sam to come to church. So we did. And we prayed every night after that. But even though Ellie continued to come, Sam continued to refrain. Over the next year, as we continued to have dinners, see movies, and even take trips together, Sam would occasionally ask questions about church, but never very many.

One Sunday, while I was teaching, I perused the congregation as I typically do. I saw Ellie sitting next to my wife, and on the other side of Ellie . . . was Sam! I tried not to burst out, "I can't believe you're here" in the middle of my message, but I was certainly stunned.

Later that afternoon, when I came home, my girls came running to greet me at the door.

"Dad! Dad! Guess who was at church today?"

"Who?"

"Sam!!!"

As great as it was to have Sam at church, it was even more

wonderful to know that my girls now knew that God answers prayers.

Sam was still pretty skeptical, though. As I continued to get to know him, it became clear that he'd had several bad experiences in his past that had led to spiritual confusion. He was rather quiet about God and the things we talked about in church, so he and I didn't talk about it much. Even though Sam started coming more often to church with Ellie and their kids, he rarely talked about it otherwise. So I just left it alone.

Until one night it came up. Finally.

We were driving home from a movie, and Sam said, "You know, I didn't really grow up religious. This is all new for me. Do you mind if I ask you some questions?"

"Sure, not a problem."

"Tell me why you believe this."

For a second, my heart stopped. If you've ever been in this situation, you know how scary it is. You've waited for it, you've prayed for it, and you've hoped for it; but when you finally have your opportunity to explain what means more to you than anything, how do you sum it up?

Maybe your friend confides in you about a marriage that is really hitting the rocks, or kids who are out of control, or a setback at work, or a diagnosis from the doctor. Your friend looks at you and says, "Your family seems to weather things a bit differently. Why is that?"

Maybe they know you go to church, and they start talking about how they went to church as a kid but hated it . . .

and then they look at you and say, "Why is it so important to you?"

In that moment, every sermon, every Christian song, every bumper sticker comes flooding back to your mind. When Sam asked me about my faith, I thought of everything from the Lamb's Book of Life to the four horsemen of the apocalypse to *The Fellowship of the Ring*.

What is the truth we share when kindness has opened the door?

Sharing the *story* of our faith will always make a bigger impact than sharing the *facts* of our faith. We love stories; we make time to see and hear stories. The same is true when sharing our faith.

> Sharing the *story* of our faith will always make a bigger impact than sharing the *facts* of our faith.

This must be what happened with the demon-possessed man whom Jesus healed in the region of the Gerasenes.[7] He lived outside the city among the tombs, and no one was strong enough to subdue him when he lost his cool. Then Jesus arrived on the scene and delivered him from his curse. As Jesus was leaving town, this newly freed man asked to come along, but Jesus said no. Instead, he told the man to go home to his family and friends and "tell them everything the Lord has done for you and how merciful he has been."[8] The next time Jesus entered that region, so many people showed up to see him that he had to provide five thousand sack lunches to feed them all.[9]

Paul captures the essence of the Good News when he declares, "The old life is gone; a new life has begun!"[10] This is a perfect model for sharing our stories: the contrast between the old and the new, between my life before Jesus and my life with Jesus.

Tell the story of what God has done for *you*. What was your life like before you knew Jesus, and what has it been like since? That's what the blind man does in John 9:1-34. After Jesus heals him of his blindness, someone asks the man a theological question about how Jesus could have done that. He replies, "I don't know. One thing I *do* know. I was blind but now I see!"[11]

The great thing about telling your own story is that you don't have to know everything about the Bible to be able to help someone connect to God.

I saw this play out with a couple in our church who had recently moved from Michigan. John was a believer, but Jeanine was far from it. Her struggle with church had been going on for years. She'd never gone to church when she was growing up, and her only perspective on church was that the people were insensitive and judgmental. To make matters worse, she'd had a roommate in college who claimed to be a Christian but had some rather unorthodox practices—such as praying to a mannequin she called Jesus. Jeanine said she never knew where the mannequin would be at night when she came home. Sometimes it was in the closet; other times it was on her bed. One time it was even in a coffin that her roommate had brought in. It was easy for Jeanine to decide that if this was Christianity, it wasn't for her.

Jeanine got married, but even though John went to church, she was never interested. Years later, they moved to Valencia. John got plugged into our church and convinced Jeanine to try it. After she came reluctantly for a few weeks in a row, John got ambitious and signed the two of them up for one of our home Bible studies. He convinced her it would be safe—eat, talk, go home. So she went.

The first night, during dinner, she got everyone's attention and declared, "I just want you all to know something: I don't believe any of the stuff you all believe."

Instead of reacting the way she thought they would, they said, "No problem. We're glad you're here." Their kindness was more than unexpected; it was shocking.

Jeanine thought the experience was too good to be true, so she kept attending to see what would happen. Over the next few months, she joined the group for everything: weekly Bible studies, serving at the homeless shelter, and holiday dinners. They even TP'd the lead pastor's house. (Thank you very much!) When the group was together, Jeanine would occasionally ask the others some questions about their faith. Their responses were simple: They shared their own stories.

After a year of this, Jeanine stopped everything once again one night at the weekly home Bible study.

"I have something I need to say," she said.

By this point, she was no longer looking at a roomful of strangers but at a group of trusted friends—friends who had shown her impeccable kindness and who had shared their life stories and faith journeys with her.

With a trembling voice she declared, "Yesterday at church I decided to become a Christian."

There wasn't a dry eye in the house. After the hugs and the tears, someone asked Jeanine what had helped her. She said, "The kindness you showed me and the stories you told me."

Later that week, when they baptized Jeanine in a hot tub in someone's backyard, the group celebrated the result of what happens when we partner with God—not through sales pitches, leaflets, or debates but simply through kindness.

> When Jesus tells us to let our light shine, it isn't to show people how blind they are or how bright we are.

I know the pushback from some believers regarding this approach is that we need to confront sin and preach doctrine, or else people won't see their need and won't know what it means to become a Christian. Other believers say that we must simply be the best example of Christ we can be, and nonbelievers will somehow understand. This is often referred to as the "brightest lightbulb" approach: If I'm a bright light in a dark world, then other people will figure it out. But this approach places all the emphasis either on us or on them. When Jesus tells us to let our light shine, it isn't to show people how blind they are or how bright we are but rather to show them the way to God. Showing kindness is a great way to turn the lights on.

I remember a quote from Dwight L. Moody, one of the more committed and successful nineteenth-century evangelists. People often criticized his methods for getting the gospel out to people, but his response was simple: "I like my way of doing it better than your way of *not* doing it."

So when my new friend Sam asked me on our way back from the movie why I believed what I believe, I said, "I believe the facts prove that Jesus rose from the dead—just as he predicted he would. If you can pull that off, I'll listen to everything else you say. And ever since I've started doing that . . . my life has been different."

> When we show people kindness, God shows them grace.

"Thanks," Sam said. "Can I ask you other questions later?"

"Of course!"

Pretty much every time we got together after that, Sam would have a few more questions about the church or God or the Bible. After about a year of asking questions, Sam asked me one night while we were out headed to a movie, "Do you think you'd mind baptizing our family?"

I almost wrecked the car, I was so excited.

"I think I could fit you into my schedule," I joked.

I'll never forget the September night when our church family gathered around Sam and Ellie's family and celebrated their baptisms. I don't know who was weeping more, but I do know the thrill of seeing the years of kindness and patience result in God's grace taking this new family.

For years I had hoped to see people experience what I had experienced through Jesus. By finally participating with God in their lives, I ultimately had that pleasure. We can't share the truth of Jesus without showing his kindness, as well. And when we show people kindness, God shows them grace.

chapter nine

WHEN YOU

PLACE YOUR HOPE

IN GOD, THEN GOD

WILL GIVE YOU

HOPE

When I arrived at Real Life Church, the church was about three years old and was still renting a local movie theater for services. It was a nice theater—I mean, it was no ArcLight, but it served our purpose at the time. The multiplex had twelve auditoriums, and we rented four of them on Sunday mornings from 6:00 a.m. to 11:30 a.m.

Every Sunday, a group of the Lord's most dedicated servants showed up at 6:00 a.m. to begin the process of converting dirty, popcorn-filled, sticky-floored theaters into worship spaces for both kids and adults. We were able to squeeze in two services—at 9:00 and 10:00—but the closing song for the 9:00 service often became the opening song for the service at 10:00. Sometimes Communion was "to go." Then, at 11:00, we had to tear it all down to be out by 11:30. There were some Sundays when we tore things down in the dark after the 11:30 movie had already started.

As you might imagine, everyone said we needed a permanent home. Whether it meant buying a piece of land and building on it or renovating an available vacant building, the overall consensus was that we needed to do something. But as challenging as our weekly logistics were, I was not yet convinced that we needed our own building. I had recently been through two capital campaigns in a row at my last church, and the thought of launching into a third was exhausting. Perhaps we could make the theater work for a while longer.

I was a bit naive.

Another thing that made the theater setup interesting was that the movies were on a set timer, and sometimes they'd come on during church. There's nothing quite like watching a remake of *The Texas Chainsaw Massacre* while trying to read the Bible. It was even more unsettling when a movie would come on in the theater that housed our nursery. There's no easy way to explain to parents that their children might have seen ten minutes of *Saw* or *The Hills Have Eyes*. Still, I wasn't convinced yet that we needed a building.

One Sunday, we had a junior-high class meeting in one of the auditoriums, and the leaders decided to play a game with the kids at the front of the theater. There's a good reason why they keep the lights off in theaters, and it's not just so you can see the screen. It's so you can't see how disgusting the floor is. But these were junior-high schoolers; they didn't care. Most of them didn't shower anyway. The game began, and the students ended up rolling around on the floor, pulling on each other and having a great time—that is, until one poor boy rolled underneath the screen. There is a small curtain that hides the gap between the bottom of the screen and the floor, and this kid rolled under it for just a moment. He really wasn't gone long. But when he returned, he created an unforgettable memory: Attached to his back was one of those sticky rat traps—complete with a dead rat.

The girls screamed in horror and the boys screamed in excitement, but the student with the rat on his back was less than thrilled. Apparently his parents weren't all that excited about it, either—we never saw them again. That was the day

I decided that maybe we should get a building of our own after all. "*When* you meet in a movie theater, *then* your kids go home wearing rats" was not the kind of When/Then we were trying to promote.

We assembled a building team to help us find a facility. We asked our people to begin praying for God to provide us with a permanent home. After a few months of looking, we found a piece of land that seemed perfect. It was not only in the center of town; it was also nestled between several housing developments that were brimming with young families. But when we went to the city to inquire about developing it, they replied rather curtly, "No. It's not zoned for a church."

We were shaken but not discouraged. We kept praying and looking.

Next, a vacant building that was right off the highway, with great visibility for thousands of cars each day, presented itself. It was a great fit for us, and it would be cheaper to renovate an existing building than to build a new one. Again we went to the city, and again city officials said no. "That's zoned for a business."

This soon became a pattern for us. We'd pray; we'd find a place; we'd go to the city; and they'd say no. I'll be honest: I was having a hard time keeping up my enthusiasm for this project, or even for our future as a church. I was beginning to wonder where God was in all of this. We were praying, and we were trying to advance his Kingdom; why was he not allowing it to happen?

After about two years of striking out, we came across

another building that we thought was a sure thing. The owner was willing to sell. We had secure funding. We even had an architect draw up some preliminary plans. All that was left was approval from the city. The night before our meeting with the city, we assembled our prayer team. We drove out to the building and walked around it seven times, praying for God's favor and for him to allow us to have this space. There was so much momentum after that night. There were so many dreams of what we could do with that space. We all drove home feeling certain that this was how God was leading us.

The next day, we went to city hall. We sat down across from a city official, who looked at our plans, heard our case, and then politely said, "Sorry, it's not zoned for a church." In the next split second, I had many thoughts go through my head—thoughts that Jesus probably wouldn't have had. *Where is God? Is there any hope?*

I know you've had this experience too. It may not have been with a church building; but maybe there was a house you wanted to purchase, and every bank kept saying no. Maybe with every pregnancy test you've taken, the results are always the same: *negative.* Perhaps you've been applying to your dream jobs, and you keep hearing, "We've decided to go in another direction." Maybe for every college application you've sent out you get a letter back saying, "No, but thank you for applying." You're left wondering, *What did I do wrong? Did I not pray enough? Is God punishing me? How do I fix this?*

For some, the *no* you received from God was about something much greater than college admission or a new home; it was about your health or the health of someone close to you. Your dad was diagnosed with cancer and you prayed for a miracle, but he still died. Your son was in an accident and you prayed for his healing, but he still suffers today. Perhaps you were diagnosed with a debilitating illness and you've prayed for years, but all you hear is silence.

We all wonder where God is at times like these. Our minds search for answers, but it's like looking for a light switch in the dark. We know there must be a reason, but we can't find it. Do we need to pray more? Do we need to pray in a different way? Is God just not there?

> Do we need to pray more? Do we need to pray in a different way? Is God just not there?

Those of us who have a Thou Shalt approach to faith are prone to believe that it's entirely our own fault. Maybe we decide to work harder, pray more, fast for several days—anything to get God's attention. Behind all our efforts is a little thought that says: "I must be able to control this." But that's not partnership.

For those of us who think this is all God's fault, we chalk it up to his distance or maybe his indifference toward us. This leads to a lack of trust and to skepticism about his love for us. Behind our frustration is an unspoken belief that says, "God owes me the outcome I want." But that is not partnership either.

Part of our confusion may come from a misunderstanding of a When/Then found in the book of Romans: "We know that God causes everything to work together for the good of those who love God and are called according to his purpose for them."[1] At first glance we might take this to mean that God *causes* every circumstance—or as some may conclude, "Everything happens for a reason." This can be devastating to those of us who are dealing with illness, misfortune, or great loss. We naturally think, *What possible reason could there be for this? Why would God do this?* This leads to a life without hope because we think that God is not good. But this verse doesn't mean that God causes every occurrence in our lives; rather, he takes whatever circumstances we face and works them together to eventually produce something good.

Here is a better way to read this verse: *Nothing can happen that God cannot redeem.*

I once heard a Chinese parable that may shed further light on this point.

One day a farmer's horse ran away. His neighbor heard the bad news and came over to commiserate.

"I hear that you lost your horse. That is bad news and bad luck."

"One cannot say for sure," said the farmer. "As of yet, it is too early to tell."

The next day, the farmer's horse returned to the stable, but it brought along a drove of wild horses it had befriended. The neighbor could not quite believe the news of his friend's good fortune.

"This is such good fortune," he said. "You have increased your herd substantially."

"One cannot say for sure," the farmer replied. "As of yet, it is too early to tell."

The next day, the farmer's son decided to ride one of the new wild horses, to break it in. But no sooner had he mounted the horse than it threw him from the saddle and broke his leg.

Upon hearing this sad news, the neighbor came over to offer condolences.

"This is such a sad thing," he said. "Your son has broken his leg. This is bad news."

"One cannot say for sure," the wise farmer replied. "As of yet, it is too early to tell."

On the following day, soldiers came by, commandeering an army. They took the neighbor's son and sons from most of the surrounding farms, but left the farmer's son behind because he had a broken leg. He was spared from a battle in which all the other young men died.

The story could go on and on, but you get the point. Nothing can be properly evaluated until the end. We have a limited vantage point, but God does not.

My wife called me one day and said, "I'm lost."

"Are you using the GPS on your phone?"

"No, can you guide me?"

I used an app on my phone that allowed me to see exactly where she was and where she was headed. I was then able to give her turn-by-turn directions that helped her get back on course. The reason I could do this? I was seeing things from the satellite's perspective, whereas she was seeing things from a street-level perspective. I had a better vantage point than she did. God has a vantage point from which he sees not only the present but also all of time.

> God has a vantage point from which he sees not only the present but also all of time.

God's sovereignty and omniscience (infinite knowledge and insight) means that we can do more than say, "It might work out great later on." Our belief is not in the karmic hope that fate will somehow even things out in the long run; our belief is that a very real and personal and resourceful God can and will bring good out of anything. Not everything happens for a reason, but everything can be redeemed.

Here's another thought on this verse: Our good is God's goal. We think that if God is going to work all things for our good, then we should enjoy every outcome. But when we lose our job or our spouse walks out on us, we can start to lose faith. This leads to a life without hope in God because we end up blaming him for our lack of pleasure or comfort. But this verse is not saying that God will cause every single event in our lives to have a positive outcome for us. He has a much larger plan than just what concerns us, and he will use all things to work together for the ultimate good he has in mind.

God's sovereignty does not mean that he causes everything or that everything that happens is his will. It was not God's will that you were injured or abused, for example. Whatever happens, happens for many reasons; but *nothing ever happens that God cannot redeem.*

What really shocks people about this verse is that this promise is not even for everyone. The assurance that God will redeem all the bad in our lives and in the world is found only in partnership with him. *When* we love him and are called according to his purpose, *then* God works things together for good. In other words, *when* we put our hope in God, *then* he provides hope for us.

> When we love him and are in the center of his will, we will eventually see how everything can be redeemed.

When we love him and are in the center of his will, we will eventually see how everything can be redeemed. That's the only way we can appreciate what he's up to.

God is less of a puppet master who controls all things and more of a director conducting a grand symphony. When we play the music he conducts, not only do the notes eventually make sense, but they also turn into beautiful music in harmony with every other part being played. That's what it means to "love God" and be "called according to his purpose."

In some ways, this idea is the culmination of every When/Then equation we've talked about. *When* we decide to respond to God's call on our lives; *when* we decide to put our trust in him; *when* we decide to walk with his Son; *when* we live with our eyes always on him; *when* we invest in his Kingdom; and *when* we show love and kindness to others so they might meet God, *then* we live in partnership with him and have placed our hope in him. As Paul says, "This hope will not lead to disappointment."[2] One day, we will see that everything—every pain, every wound, every loss, every mistake, every fear, every destructive habit, every abuse, every hurtful word—can and will be redeemed.

Sometimes we even get to see the good that God is orchestrating.

I remember as if it were yesterday sitting in the city official's office for the final time. When he said for the umpteenth time, "Sorry, it's not zoned for a church," it was as if my heart had been ripped from my chest. Trying my best not to say what was running through my mind, I suddenly sensed the Holy Spirit taking over. Looking across the desk with what must have been eyes of desperation, I said, "If not there . . . then *where?*"

"Excuse me?"

I tried not to act as surprised as he was. I said, "For the past two years, every idea we have, every building we find, every piece of land that might work, we bring it to you and your answer is always the same: *No*. Is there any place you could say *yes* to?"

He thought for a long while and said, "Well, now that you mention it, there is a piece of property that was just recently rezoned. I think you could build a church there."

My jaw hit the floor. "Where would that be?" I asked.

When he told us the location, I nearly passed out. What he didn't know was that he had just given me the address for the very first piece of land we had ever looked at—two years earlier. It was as if God had said, "Right place, wrong time." And truth be told, we would not have been able to afford, develop, or raise capital for that property two years earlier. We live life moving forward, but often we see God's hand by looking back.

> We live life moving forward, but often we see God's hand by looking back.

Two years later—just as we were knee-deep in our building project, our church was growing, and excitement for the building was rising—the recession hit. Suddenly, people who had made big pledges of financial support were losing their jobs. Their 401(k)s had become 201(k)s. Homes were being lost. Everyone was scared, including me. We were already having to pay on the loan for the building, but our income was decreasing. How were we going to do this? We had taken a risk, we had stepped out in faith, we'd been obedient to God . . . and now, what was this? Would it all be for naught? Would we default on the construction loan before we even moved in to the building? And would our failure to complete the project become a black eye on the church in our city?

As the year drew to a close, we needed to raise $1 million by the end of December. This seemed like an impossible task. I began to ask, "God, how could this be for *anyone's* good?"

One morning, I got a call from one of our staff members, who said, "There's this new guy at the church who would like to have lunch with you."

I thought, *I've got enough problems I can't solve. I don't need to go to lunch with someone and try to solve his!*

But I went.

We exchanged small talk for a while and traded details about each other's history and journey to California. Then he said, "I've got a question for you."

Here we go, I thought.

"My wife and I have been checking out this church for a while, trying to see if this is where God wants us. We love the building project and we love the work you're doing in Africa, and we'd like to be part of this."

"Great!"

Then he completely shocked me. "We feel as if God is prompting us to give a large gift to the building project that might motivate others. We'd like for this gift to be used as a matching fund. If you can find a few others to help, we could match up to $500,000."

It was at that moment that I decided to pick up the tab for lunch.

Over the next six weeks, God used this couple's gift in such a powerful way that we were able to raise $1.1 million and keep the project going. Their act of generosity motivated others to give and motivated our leadership team to have faith. If we hadn't been in such dire straits, that gift would not have had nearly the impact it had.

When we finally opened the building and saw thousands pour in for the first time, it was one of those moments when you just *knew* God had worked everything together for good—the good of all those who gave; the good of all those who began coming to the church; the good of all those who had served for ten years, waiting on that day; and certainly the good of the Kingdom of God. Sometimes we are privileged to see God's purpose as it comes to fruition.

> Sometimes we are privileged to see God's purpose as it comes to fruition. . . . Sometimes we won't see the good until the next life.

Of course, sometimes we won't see the good until the next life.

If there was anyone who was excited about our building, it was Mike Davis. As a realtor in our valley, he had been selling houses and helping people for at least twenty years. He had a great reputation as one of the nicest, most loyal, and most dedicated people you'd ever know. He was dedicated to the Lord, to his family, and to Real Life Church. Mike and his family had joined RLC on the day it had launched, and they hadn't looked back.

It wasn't hard to find Mike. He was always there. When our church was meeting in the movie theater, he was there early to set out the Communion elements and sweep up bits of popcorn that had been missed. When people started to arrive, he walked around greeting everyone and helping them to their seats. He made his own name tag that he wore every Sunday so people knew whom to ask if they had questions. When the worship music began, he'd stand in the theater clapping and singing yet keeping an eye on the door in case any latecomers needed help finding a seat.

Mike and I had lunch together every two months or so, and during our search for a building site, he'd always have an idea about where we could buy land. He'd take me by an open field and say, "Can you see it? Thousands coming to this spot to hear about Jesus!" Mike was one of those guys who could see things long before the rest of us could.

When we finally purchased land, he was one of the first people I notified. He was so excited he could hardly stand it. "Rusty, this is going to be huge for this city!" As the building's completion drew closer, he would randomly call me with ideas for mailers to send out to the neighbors and to the list of people who he was praying would attend on opening day. He couldn't wait to be there.

Several months before the building was finished, Mike was diagnosed with leukemia. Our staff gathered around to pray and cry together. "God, please spare Mike. He's been so faithful to you. Would you please heal him?"

Over the next few months, we visited with him and prayed for him. Every time I saw him in the hospital, he'd introduce me to every nurse, doctor, and attendant who was working with him. He'd assure me that he'd invited them to church, and they had promised him that they would be there for the first day in the new building. I'd thank him and pray for him, and while leaving the hospital I would beg God to spare Mike's life. I couldn't imagine Real Life Church without Mike Davis.

Despite all the prayers from everyone who knew Mike, God took him home barely a month before we opened the building. We all were stunned. How could this be? What good could come from this? On the day of Mike's funeral, hundreds of people poured into a small chapel in town to pay their respects to this amazing man. Many of the people who shared about his life weren't Christians, but they didn't hesitate to talk about Mike's faith. Mike had made an eternal impact on them that they didn't even realize until he was gone. I had the privilege to speak about Mike and his faith at the funeral service. When I said I was Mike's pastor at Real Life Church, there was a collective gasp from the audience— as if everyone who wasn't a part of our church realized at the same moment, *Oh,* this *is the guy from the church he kept talking about!*

The big day finally came, and we moved into our long-awaited building. It was such a fun day, filled with tears and hugs and excitement. But there was some sadness along with all the joy. Mike wasn't there. Several of us stood off to one side and took a few moments to reminisce about Mike's life. We knew that if he had been there, he would have been running around welcoming everyone, picking up trash, and telling everyone who was serving what a great job they were doing. As we stood watching thousands of people file through our doors, someone said, "He would have loved to see this!" Then someone else said, "Not only is he seeing it . . . he saw it long before we did!"

Over the next few months, the church grew exponentially. There were so many Sundays when I'd be standing in the lobby greeting all the new people, and I'd ask them how they had heard about the church. I lost track of the number of times I heard, "Mike Davis invited me."

We also had the privilege of baptizing hundreds of people in our first few years in the building. Often when I stood in the baptistery, people would tell me, "I never really considered church until Mike Davis's funeral. But now, here I am. And now I'm ready to be baptized."

I like to think that Mike could see that, or at least that Jesus told him about it. *When* Mike put his hope in God years ago, *then* God gave him the hope that everything could be redeemed. And redemption is what we saw even as we grieved the loss of our friend.

THE WHEN/THEN PARTNERSHIP LIFE

chapter ten

I'm sure you've heard some of the stories about the hilarious calls received by computer help desks. Well-meaning people trying to use their computers often struggle to understand the basics of the technology. For instance, there's the story of a woman who was told to close all her windows, so she got up from the computer and closed all the windows in the house. One man was frustrated when his computer's coffee-cup holder broke—only to discover that the "mug holder" was actually a disc tray.

We may enjoy a good laugh at their expense, but the truth is that we've all been guilty of using a good thing in the wrong way. Are you saying you've never used your teeth to open a package, a butter knife to turn screws, or a shoe to hammer nails? I doubt it's just me.

I've even gone so far as to (unwittingly) mislead others to use a good thing for the wrong reason.

Several years ago on Halloween, my wife and I decided to line our driveway with a decoration involving brown paper sacks and candles. This type of lantern has a variety of names, but it's simple to make: You take a brown paper lunch sack, fill it with a bit of dirt or sand, nestle a candle inside, and light it up. Then you line your walkway with these lanterns, and you have a collection of lights leading people up to your front door for trick-or-treating.

We went to great lengths to prepare the bags ahead of time, using battery-powered tea lights to maintain fire safety, and I put them out on the front porch until it was time to set them up and turn them on. Having completed this project, I began helping my wife to get the kids ready for some trick-or-treating of our own. The plan was to hit a few houses on our street and then come home, light up our driveway, and pass out our own candy. With all the excitement of the evening, the difficulty of assembling butterfly and princess costumes, and the rush to get out the door, I forgot about the big box of brown paper sacks on our front porch.

When we returned about an hour later, the box on the porch was empty.

"Who would take my lanterns?" I wondered.

At about the same moment, I began receiving sarcastic text messages from neighbors and friends.

"Hey, thanks a lot for the bag of dirt!"

"Looks like you went for trick instead of treat this year."

"I've heard of wax *lips* for Halloween, but a candle?"

I was embarrassed, yet amused, as I thought of my many neighbors sending their kids to our door, thinking we'd left out treats . . .

It's not that the lanterns were a bad idea; they were just used in the wrong way.

Unfortunately, we Christians have a way of doing this with the things of Jesus. For instance, Communion was a great idea until it turned into a drunken brawl in Corinth.[1] Doing good deeds, such as giving money to the poor, was a noble endeavor until the church tied the giving of alms to the granting of indulgences to limit a person's punishment for sin. Baptism, another beautiful sacrament, reflected a powerful connection with God until some churches made it seem as if the water were more responsible for our salvation than Jesus was. Church services can be a visible congregation of the bride of Christ, or they can become lifeless prisons where we do our time each week to earn God's favor. Even the Bible— the sacred Scriptures, the Word of God—has been used to create power struggles.

Likewise, many of the Bible's When/Thens have been used in the wrong way.

Some of us have felt the pain that results when people take God's promises and invitations and turn them into a collection of Thou Shalts—either imposing guilt on those who fail to keep all the commands perfectly, or creating avoidance in those who are afraid to even try. When God's Word is presented as a to-do list from an angry cosmic judge who is just waiting for us to mess up so he can smack us down, it can turn even the best of us into legalists who keep track of our progress and the progress of others. Some of us know that pain all too well. We were raised in homes or churches that used God's Word as a battering ram, and we received condemnation and shame for our lack of effort, progress, or success.

But the Bible is not meant to be used as a blunt-force instrument. It is filled with encouragement, good news, grace, and possibilities. It is filled with invitations to join God in fulfilling his mission in the world. It is filled with

> Many of the Bible's When/Thens have been used in the wrong way.

opportunities to partner with God in a fruitful relationship and in life transformation.

Some of us know firsthand the consequences of ignoring God's promises and invitations because we've viewed God's Word as ancient literature that no longer applies to us. We live with regrets, wishing we had accepted Christ or decided to follow biblical principles earlier in life. If only we had done that, it might have saved our first marriage, or provided boundaries for our kids, or shaped our financial decisions.

Some of us have felt the sting of seeing those we love view the commands of God as a bunch of Never Minds, and they keep wrecking their lives and wondering why. Yet some of us are the negligent ones. We read words such as "I can do all things through Christ who strengthens me"[2] or "The LORD is my shepherd, I shall not want"[3] and see them as taglines for a motivational poster with a sunset or a litter of kittens.

But the Bible is so much more than a collection of inspirational statements. It is filled with real-life wisdom, warnings, and guidance. It is filled with invitations for us to change the world rather than simply exist. It is filled with directions that can help us steer clear of the potholes and pitfalls that threaten to ruin our lives and the lives of those we love.

"I Never Noticed That Before . . ."

If you're at all like me, your view of God's Word may have drifted over the years without you even noticing. When I realized one day how much my perspective had shifted, it changed my life.

Have you ever had an "I never noticed that before" moment? It may have been with a restaurant in a strip mall near your house, or a scratch on the side of your car, or the gray hairs quietly infiltrating your head. We've all had at least one "when did that happen?" experience with common things in our lives that we somehow overlooked. Some of us have even had such an experience with the Bible. Truth be told, it has happened to me many times. I'm reading along and suddenly I see something I haven't noticed before.

"When did they sneak *that* verse in there?"

"Has that always been there?"

"How did I overlook that?"

A few years ago, during my daily time of reading in the Bible, I came across a passage that greatly affected my life.

I thought I'd seen it all. I grew up going to church three or four times a week, and when you're there that often, you cover a lot of ground in the Bible. When I went to a Christian college, the Bible was one of my textbooks. After graduation I became a pastor, and the Bible became my employee handbook. And yet after all those years spent reading the Bible, one day I noticed something I'd never seen before. It was something so huge, so dramatic, and so significant that it changed everything for me.

I found this passage near the end of the Sermon on the Mount. Jesus is finishing up his amazing message to his disciples and everyone else who has come to hear him speak. He has encouraged them; he has challenged them; he has clarified his relationship to the law they'd been taught to keep all their lives; and he has even given some specific When/Then statements for everyone to ponder. He has tackled some heavy topics—including marriage, divorce, revenge, anger, commitments, justice, and worry, just to name a few—but it's the conclusion to his message that really shook me up.

After using a variety of illustrations throughout his sermon, he tells a simple story about two house builders. One guy builds his house on the beach. Though we all might love to have some oceanfront property, the unique thing about this man's design is that there was no firm foundation, just walls up on the sand. Some people might call this camping. And sure enough, as soon as a good storm came up and the tide rolled in, the house was reduced to a pile of sticks.

The other guy decided to build his house on a rock overlooking the ocean. He picked out a strong, flat formation to use as his foundation, and he built from there. His place may have been a bit farther from the water, but it was secure. It was anchored to the rock. When that same storm blew through, the house was unshakable.[4]

I guess I'd heard so many sermons imploring me not to build my house on the sand—the "how not to"—that I had missed the "how to." In this wrap-up to the greatest message ever preached, Jesus tells us not only how to avoid the sand, but also how to build our lives on the rock: "Everyone who hears these words of mine and puts them into practice . . ."

Here's how I used to read that sentence: "Everyone who

hears these words of mine . . ." That was all. So I made it
my mission to *hear* more. I took classes, joined groups, and
learned all the methods of biblical study and exegesis. My
entire life revolved around consuming more and more knowledge. I double-majored at Bible college. I went to seminary.
I spent much of my time in Christian bookstores or discuss-
ing books about God. I enrolled in
seminars and conferences, and I even
got a subscription that allowed me to
hear more sermons than just the ones
I heard at church on Sunday. I took
notes on everything—and kept them.
I put pages upon pages in three-ring
binders and collected journals on my
shelves. When it came to knowledge,
I had it. I had *heard* the Word of God.

> What I had missed . . .
> was the second half
> of the statement:
> "Everyone who hears
> these words of mine and
> puts them into practice."

But what I had missed, and what I finally noticed, was
the second half of that statement: "Everyone who hears these
words of mine *and puts them into practice.*"

Wait—what? How had I missed that for so long?

It wasn't enough to study; it wasn't enough to learn; it
wasn't enough to gain knowledge. I had to *use* what I learned.
I had to put it into action; I had to put it into practice. Truth
be told, though all the knowledge I had acquired might have
made me *smarter*, it hadn't necessarily made me *wiser*. In fact,
some of the things I had studied and read and written down
were the same things I had heard and learned and recorded
years earlier. I just failed to recognize it because all of my

knowledge was collected, processed, and categorized but never applied.

In the years since this stunning revelation, I've noticed that I'm not the only one who has failed to read the entire verse in Matthew 7:24. In fact, this is where many followers of Jesus have gotten stuck. It turns out they've been learning a lot about Jesus but not really following him. Many longtime Christians, and even some new ones, become consumed with acquiring knowledge about their faith, but then they wonder why they still have all the same struggles, the same fears, and the same temptations. They begin to wonder whether they've done something wrong or whether God isn't holding up his end of the bargain. In other words, they wonder, "Whose fault is it?"

The answer they come up with usually falls into one of three categories: "It's God's fault!" "It's my fault!" or "It's the church's fault!"

"It's God's fault!"

This response is based on the (faulty) assumption that God is supposed to take away all temptation, shore up all our weaknesses, remove all our doubts, heal all our sicknesses, and clear all paths to our financial, emotional, physical, and vocational success. After all, we've spent a lot of time reading his Word.

"It's my fault!"

We just need to learn more, get another Bible study on our calendar, or maybe learn Greek and possibly even Hebrew.

Whatever it takes. Is Aramaic really a dead language? We can learn it if we need to; it might help.

"It's the church's fault!"

If the pastor would just yell more, scold more, or educate more, then he'd preach the sin right out of us. Or if the church would just offer a few more programs or a few more studies, then we'd all immediately turn into the pictures of perfection God had in mind when he created us. When we assume that it's the church's responsibility to do everything for us, we'll always be "church shopping." No place will ever be enough because it was never intended to be enough.

Here's the problem: If education were the issue, Satan would probably be a great disciple. He knows more than all of us. Though education is necessary, the issue is bigger than that.

While the Bible makes it clear that Jesus is the only way to God and that it is his free gift of grace that brings us back to God, it also makes it clear that, once we are saved, we live in partnership with God. And though we stand in grace, we live by faith. James says that faith without good deeds is dead. In other words, Jesus has saved us, but for a purpose—not just to give us a get-out-of-hell-free card.

I once heard pastor Randy Frazee tell a story of inviting the great theologian J. I. Packer to his church to observe their discipleship process. After spending some time with their church, Packer said, "You know what your problem is? Your church studies the Bible too much." Frazee was a bit stunned.

Packer concluded, "Your people are in five Bible studies a week but have no dirt under their nails from working with the poor."

Our ability to build a house on the rock is based not on what we learn but on what we do with what we've learned. Our opportunity to have an unshakable life when storms come has less to do with what we've made note of and more to do with what we've made happen. Our participation with God is based not on how much we know but rather on how much we apply what we know.

When we hear the Word of God *and* put it into practice, then God builds an unshakable life in us. But what makes our participation with God difficult in fulfilling his plan for our lives is that it requires some dirt under our fingernails. It requires sacrifices.

> When we hear the word of God *and* put it into practice, then God builds an unshakable life in us.

All good things take a level of personal sacrifice. You want to be healthy? You have to give up some of the foods you love. You want to retire? You have to give up some of the impulse buying you do now. The same is true with the When/Thens of God. When we take some risks, when we make some sacrifices, we not only partner with God in his mission but also build an unshakable life—one that won't collapse when the storms come our way.

Jesus consistently taught this way of thinking. Fast-forward a couple of years in his life and people are still talking about him, still learning about him, and still drawing conclusions about who he is. (Simply put, Jesus was still trending!) And then Jesus says: "If any of you wants to be my follower, you must turn from your selfish ways, take up your cross, and follow me."[5] He's still talking about sacrifice and the cost of discipleship.

It's not enough just to know about Jesus or to feel good about Jesus or to learn what he says. You have to *do* what he says as well.

Now fast-forward several decades after Jesus has ascended to heaven, and his followers are still saying the same thing. John, one of Jesus' closest friends, says: "If you claim to follow him, then you should do what he did."[6]

My friend and fellow teaching pastor Mike Breaux refers to the integrated parts of our faith as the golf-swing approach. I'm not a very good golfer, but I do understand that there are two key parts to the swing: backswing and follow-through. Each is equally important. In order to get the ball to go where you want it to, you must have a good backswing and a good follow-through. If you have only a backswing, you'll never hit the ball. If you have only a follow-through, there will be no power.

> There are two parts to our partnership with God, as well. *Hear* the Word of God. *Do* the Word of God.

There are two parts to our partnership with God, as well. *Hear* the Word of God. *Do* the Word of God.

When we only *hear* the Word of God, we're like golfers

frozen over the tee with the club poised motionless in the air. There's no activity, no action, no contact, no advancement.

Some of us, it seems, are afraid to take a swing. We fear for our safety on a mission trip. We fear rejection from our neighbors if we invite them to church. We use excuses in serving the poor: "I don't believe in giving a handout but a hand up." All the while we do nothing.

Some others of us look like we want to take a swing . . . *at* someone! We're walking around with our clubs, just waiting for anyone who might want to debate us, contradict our beliefs, or not vote the way we think they should. This might be why so many non-Christians think Christians are judgmental. Maybe they've been hit by a nine iron. The apostle Paul puts it this way: "Knowledge puffs up while love builds up."[7]

On the other hand, when we only *do* what the Word of God says but spend little time studying it, we can be like a golfer who tries to hit the ball with no backswing. There is no power, no torque, no distance. We'd be lucky to have the ball travel more than ten feet. The same is true when we go too long without God's Word breathing new life into us. Our intentions may be good, but we don't have enough instruction. We don't know how to love people the way Christ does. We get all goofed up with a lack of boundaries. Our emotions play tricks on us and tell us to do *more* when we should be learning what to do *first*.

Some of us just keep giving and serving and volunteering. We join cause after cause after cause, never quite knowing what God wants us to do because we haven't spent any time listening to him. We just do everything ourselves. We want to change the world, but we haven't yet allowed our personal worlds to be changed. This may be why so many Christians give up, feeling defeated and like failures.

I heard this quotation recently: "Spiritual maturity is directly related to the length of time between hearing the Word of God and doing it."

Let's apply this principle to our When/Thens.

When it comes to trusting Jesus, how long does it take you to say yes to what he tells you to do? Once you're certain that you're hearing his voice, how long does it take you to follow his prompting? Are you a believer who has yet to be obedient in baptism? Are you aware of the Holy Spirit in your life, gently nudging you, but you keep ignoring him? How easy is it for you to find excuses when it comes to taking a risk for God?

What about walking with Jesus—spending time not just reading the Bible but applying it? How long does it take for you to turn Jesus' direction into action? For instance, is it getting any easier to apologize when you've wronged someone? Are you able to admit your mistakes more quickly? What about forgiveness—is it any easier? How easy is it for you to practice truth telling? Do you find that your selfishness is decreasing and your humility increasing? Would your family think of you as someone who walks with Jesus or who just believes in Jesus?

How about relaxing and putting your future in God's

hands? Are you learning how to seek first the Kingdom of God? How long does it take you to shift your devotion from your own kingdom to his? Does your mind increasingly drift toward the advancement of God's purposes, or do you always dwell on your own desires and concerns? Have you noticed that you worry less about yourself as your devotion to God's agenda increases?

What about noticing God's presence in your daily life? When he invites you to look for him in everything you encounter, do you take him up on his offer to reveal himself? How often do you notice his handiwork? How quickly are you able to attribute the work of God to the hand of God? When you have a disagreement with someone, how long does it take for you to stop trying to prove you're right and instead start seeing the image of God in the other person? As you've taken time to notice God throughout the day, have you begun to feel closer to him?

> When God invites you to look for him in everything you encounter, do you take him up on his offer to reveal himself?

Now that you've learned about God's direction to surrender your finances to him, how does your budget reflect your new understanding and commitment? Are you still spending whatever you want and giving God the leftovers? When you receive your paycheck, how long does it take for you to think about how to be generous with it? Do you find yourself noticing how God has blessed you, or are you still focused on what you lack? Do you think first about what you'll buy for yourself, or are you becoming more generous and finding new and creative ways to give even more to honor God's Kingdom?

What about sharing your faith? Do you know your neighbors' names? Have you started praying for them? Do you see your coworkers as godless pagans whom you can't wait to get away from at the end of the day, or have you chosen to see them as people whom Jesus loves and died for? How quick are you to show kindness and grace?

What about your hope? How quick are you to believe that God can bring good out of bad? How long does it take for you to convince yourself that anything can be redeemed?

How is your spiritual maturity? That is, how long is the lag time between hearing the Word of God and doing it?

Rather than waiting for more teaching or hoping for more power, maybe we should hear what God has called us to do and simply do it. We know we are called to honor our parents and our spouse, love our neighbors, confess our sin, serve the poor, and share our faith. We don't need to wait for a new Word; the Word has already been given. Doing what God has called us to is what it means to follow Jesus.

As we do that, we'll not only grow in our faith and live in partnership with our heavenly Father, but we'll also build an unshakable life.

At Real Life Church, we have small group Bible studies that meet in homes. We call these Life Groups. I'm always encouraged when I hear stories from our Life Groups about how they are putting into practice the things we talk about during our weekend services.

After one sermon series in which we talked about generosity toward people in need, our Life Groups began to ask the question, *Whom can we help, and how?*

One Life Group member knew of a neighbor who had recently had a death in the family. This family had already been struggling financially, and now with the added funeral expenses and loss of income, they were facing new challenges to go along with their grief. Upon hearing this story, the Life Group decided to have a garage sale and give all the money they collected to this hurting family. When they showed up with an envelope of money, the look on the family's faces was thanks enough.

Another Life Group knew of a woman, a single mom, whose car was in desperate need of repairs, yet she was unable to pay for them. So a mechanic in our church donated his time and talent, while the members of the Life Group used the proceeds from their own garage sale to pay for the parts. Not only did this single mom have a car that now ran, but she also experienced the love and support of a group of Jesus followers.

Yet another Life Group saw the need of a widowed father struggling to provide for his two teenage daughters, one of whom had special needs. They lived in a run-down trailer that desperately needed some accessibility updates for the disabled daughter. The group stopped by one day and assessed the needs. On the following weekend, they showed up with supplies and a crew to overhaul the entire trailer, providing an amazing, updated space. On top of that, they pulled together some money to buy a prom dress for the elder daughter.

When we hear, obey, and take action, then God changes not only *our* world but the *entire* world.

> When we hear, obey, and take action, then God changes not only *our* world but the *entire* world.

It has been only a few years since I sat in Shane's church in Vegas and came face-to-face with the realizations that I did not love God and that I was pretty sure he didn't love me. But now that I not only *know* but actually *feel* the truth about God's boundless love—for me and for the world—I walk in a new and true freedom that I have never before experienced. It has been a journey filled with ups and downs and highs and lows—it's life, after all—but through it all, I've come to hear more clearly (and more often) God's loving invitations to live the life he's provided. No longer do I sense a need to try to *earn* his love. The Cross of Jesus Christ tells me that I'm already enough as-is. No longer do I drift toward ineffectiveness by thinking that God has checked out from the story.

Recently, I was invited on a fly-fishing trip in Montana. I'm not much of a fisherman, but I was promised the opportunity to spend time with fifteen other leaders from around the country who would help me in my personal leadership. I couldn't resist. For three days, I spent eight hours a day in a boat with at least one other person as we drifted along the beautiful Bighorn River. There were bald eagles above us, blue herons along the shore, and rainbow trout swimming beneath us. It was like living in a postcard.

But it was crowded in the boat. We'd bump into each other, we'd tangle lines, we'd hook each other on the cast. But we also took pictures for each other, helped net the fish when we caught them, and shared stories about our lives that I'll never forget.

On our last evening together, we began sharing around the table what God had done in our lives over the course of the week. Some of the men talked of friendship, others of rest, and some of God's creation. One new friend in particular quoted a passage from an author named Hafiz:

> *God*
> *And I have become*
> *Like two giant fat people*
> *Living in a*
> *Tiny boat.*
> *We*
> *Keep*
> *Bumping into each other and*
> *Laughing.*[8]

While everyone else laughed, I started to cry. This was my greatest discovery. After three days in a boat with someone else, I was beginning to believe that God really is in the boat of life with me. And he is pleased to be there. And we just keep bumping into each other as we try to row this thing in the right direction. And every time we do, we laugh.

My prayer for you is that you will awaken to the truth of your presence in God's boat.

And that you will keep bumping into each other.

And laughing.

discussion guide

This discussion guide will help you go deeper in personally applying Rusty's message of jumping in and fully trusting God with your life. Invite others—your spouse, coworkers, or a church group—to join you, or use this guide on your own for individual reflection. Though it is structured as a four-week study, feel free to adapt it for a shorter or longer time to suit your needs. For more resources, visit www.whenyouthengod.com.

· · • **Week 1** • · ·
Read Chapters 1 and 2

Chapter 1: Ready to Jump?

1. As Rusty says, "Jumping can be scary business." Describe a time when you had to take a leap of faith. What were some of the fears holding you back from jumping? What happened after you jumped?

2. What about when you've jumped and fallen? Are you afraid that your failure is an indication of God's anger or punishment? How can you remind yourself of the truth of God's provision and help others to remember as well?

3. Rusty suggests that we can't fully trust God until we understand his love for us. What are some tangible ways in which you feel God's delight in you and his love for you? What are some things that keep you from feeling and *believing* God's love?

4. Rusty's longtime friend Shane is able to see what Rusty's spiritual life is really missing when they meet in Las Vegas. Do you have a friend who knows and speaks into your life like this? How can we lovingly provide this kind of support for one another?

Chapter 2: Thou Shalts and Never Minds

1. What do you think when you hear the phrase "the unconditional love of God?" Do you believe it's too good to be true?

2. Rusty admits that much of his Christian walk consisted of following a list of "Thou Shalts and Thou Shalt Nots." How has your own faith been affected by this list? Are there areas of your life where you still subscribe to the belief that God's love is conditional?

3. On the other hand, Rusty asserts that some people may subscribe to a list of "Never Minds" and often don't take

biblical principles seriously. Are there any areas of your life where you pick and choose which parts of the Bible to obey?

4. Do you feel as if you can ever do enough for God? What are some ways we can remind each other of the important truth of God's unconditional love?

5. Though we serve a God who loves us unconditionally, Rusty suggests that "the problem with seeing God's blessings as unconditional is that we assume he is obligated to do what we say, give us what we ask, and change our world—with or without our participation." How do you see this seed of entitlement in your own life? Are there ways to combat this growing problem?

· · • **Week 2** • · ·
Read Chapters 3, 4, and 5

Chapter 3: When you trust God's love, then God will invite you to partner with him

1. When Rusty talked with people about their faith, he found himself wondering, *Why not me?* Do you struggle with comparisons when you look at the faith journeys of others? On what basis do you believe that their faith experience is more important or successful than yours?

2. What slice of the "trust pie" are you keeping from God? Why are you afraid of entrusting that piece of your life to him?

3. Rusty realized that one of the major hindrances to his trust in God was "a disconnect between what I *knew* and what I actually *believed*." Do you see a similar disconnect in your own life? What are some practical ways you can work to close the gap?

4. How would your life look different if you took God at his word—believing that he loves you deeply and unconditionally? What do you have to lose?

5. Is there anything holding you back from believing that God is a When/Then God? Explain.

Chapter 4: When you walk with Jesus, then God will help you look like Jesus

1. Have you ever encountered someone who "dressed like Jesus" but didn't act like him? Have you ever been that person yourself? Describe the situation and how you felt at the time.

2. Was there ever an area or characteristic in your life that you waited on God to fix? How did you come to realize that God desires teamwork for transformation?

3. What is one way in which you'd like your life to look a little more like Jesus' life? What are some practical steps you can take toward that goal?

4. What are some ways that you abide in Jesus? As you listen to the answers of others in your group, are there any new ideas you would like to implement in your own life?

Chapter 5: *When you relax, then God will guide you*

1. Would you describe yourself as a worrier? What are some recurring fears that keep you up at night? Are there any Bible verses you've memorized that help calm you down? Explain.

2. How do you find the balance between working hard and trusting God? How do you keep your concern about the future from ruining your enjoyment of the present moment?

3. Describe a time in your life when you found yourself faced with a need for repentance and a completely new mind-set. What made you realize this, and how has your life changed since? What does *repentance* mean to you?

4. Rusty describes God as *omnipotent*, *omniscient*, and *omnibenevolent*. Which of these characteristics do you have the hardest time connecting with? Which do you believe wholeheartedly? Why?

5. What is your biggest argument for not giving God complete control of your life? How can you work to remember the truth of God's person and provision?

6. Rusty suggests that we worry only about what we are truly devoted to. What are some things you're devoted to? How can we help each other refocus on our devotion to God's Kingdom instead of our everyday worries?

· · • **Week 3** • · ·
Read Chapters 6, 7, and 8

Chapter 6: When you notice God, then God will reveal his presence

1. After a horrifyingly embarrassing incident at the local pool, Rusty realizes that he may be guilty of overlooking the details in his life. Have you ever been in a situation where missing the "fine print" cost you in the end? What did you learn from the experience?

2. Even after God proves himself faithful in a certain area of your life, are you ever left wondering whether he will show up the next time a difficult situation arises? How can we support each other in remembering God's faithfulness?

3. Rusty lays out four primary avenues by which we notice God: Scripture, creation, people, and circumstances. Where is it easiest for you to notice God's goodness? Where is it most difficult?

4. In what ways do you see yourself subscribing to the "happiness" or "siren" theories of noticing God? How can you partner with God to notice his ever-present nearness when making decisions?

5. How has God revealed himself to you lately? Share and celebrate these instances.

Chapter 7: *When you invest in God's Kingdom, then God will invest in yours*

1. Using the example of his daughters and their sand castles, Rusty suggests that "we all have something we're building and trying to maintain." What does your kingdom look like? Who's a part of it?

2. In what ways are you managing your own kingdom instead of investing in it as a part of God's Kingdom? What fears are holding you back from investing?

3. How do you see God investing in your kingdom right now? Where is he showing up?

4. As we give, God promises that he will bless us. Where have you been blessed recently as a result of your giving? What stops you from giving more?

Chapter 8: *When you show kindness to others, then God will show them grace*

1. As Rusty says, we've all had thrilling, transcendent experiences that we can't wait to share with the world—even if it was just a great meal or a new movie. What's the last thing you experienced that you couldn't wait to tell people about? What made it so great?

2. Though we're often itching to share our latest recommendations and experiences, we struggle to share our relationship with Jesus. What are some reasons that keep you from sharing?

3. Who in your life would you like to see come to Christ? Is there a practical way you can partner with God this week to reach out and share part of your faith?

4. How can we work together to extend kindness to those around us in the coming weeks?

5. What is your own story of faith?

· · · **Week 4** · · ·
Read Chapters 9 and 10

Chapter 9: *When you place your hope in God, then God will give you hope*

1. Have you ever wanted something, prayed about it, and then gotten discouraged as you waited for it to come to pass? What kept your hope alive? Did your prayer ever come to fruition?

2. How do you feel when you receive a *no* from God? How do you cope and remember God's goodness?

3. What's wrong with the phrase "Everything happens for a reason"? Is there another approach we can take when people experience hardship?

4. Rusty suggests that "God is less of a puppet master who controls all things and more of a director conducting a grand symphony." Do you believe this is true? How have your experiences informed your belief?

5. Have you ever pursued a dream only to have it seem as if God said, "Right place, wrong time"? Describe the situation and how it was resolved.

Chapter 10: The When/Then partnership life

1. As you look back on this journey, which When/Then statement resounds most powerfully with you? Which statement do you struggle to believe?

2. How has your view of the Bible changed while reading *When You, Then God*?

3. When it comes to trusting Jesus, how long does it take you to activate your faith? How can we support one another in making our trust more second nature?

4. Having read *When You, Then God*, how has your faith been strengthened in the belief that God truly loves you? What will you now do with this belief?

notes

CHAPTER 1: READY TO JUMP?

1. 1 John 4:18, NIV.
2. Kyle Gardner, chapel address, Ozark Christian College, Joplin, MO, December 1991.
3. NIV.

CHAPTER 2: THOU SHALTS AND NEVER MINDS

1. Matthew 19:16-22.
2. James 1:27.
3. Exodus 20:1-17.
4. Mark 12:28.
5. Mark 12:29-31.
6. Romans 6:1-2.

CHAPTER 3: WHEN YOU TRUST GOD'S LOVE, THEN GOD WILL INVITE YOU TO PARTNER WITH HIM

1. I owe much to Dr. John Walker and his ministry through Blessing Ranch.
2. Philippians 2:12-13.
3. Philippians 1:5, NIV.
4. Exodus 15:26.
5. 2 Chronicles 7:14.
6. John 14:9, author's paraphrase.
7. John 11:40, author's paraphrase.
8. Ephesians 2:8-9.
9. Romans 10:9.
10. Matthew 5:45, NIV.

CHAPTER 4: WHEN YOU WALK WITH JESUS, THEN GOD WILL HELP YOU LOOK LIKE JESUS

1. Galatians 5:22-23, esv.
2. Psalm 1:1-3, niv.
3. Jeremiah 17:5-8.
4. John 15:1-17.
5. John 15:5, italics added.
6. Psalm 80:8-9.
7. Psalm 80:9-11.
8. Psalm 80:12-13, 16.
9. Isaiah 5:2, 7, niv.
10. Isaiah 5:5-6, niv.
11. No one has taught me more about these things than Dallas Willard. You can read more of his thoughts on discipleship as being with Jesus and learning to be like him in *The Spirit of the Disciplines* and *The Divine Conspiracy.*
12. 1 John 2:3-6.
13. Mark 16:15.
14. Psalm 1:3, niv.

CHAPTER 5: WHEN YOU RELAX, THEN GOD WILL GUIDE YOU

1. 1 Peter 5:6-7, author's paraphrase.
2. See Proverbs 3:5-6; Matthew 11:28-30; John 14:27; Philippians 4:6-7.
3. Philippians 4:6-7.
4. Matthew 6:25-34.
5. Proverbs 12:11, niv.
6. Proverbs 14:23, niv.
7. Proverbs 20:13, niv.
8. Matthew 25:14-30.
9. Matthew 4:17, niv.
10. See Matthew 6:25, 31, niv.
11. Exodus 20:13, niv.
12. 1 Thessalonians 5:17.
13. Matthew 6:25-34, niv.
14. Thanks to Andy Stanley for explaining this concept in his message titled "Why Worry, Part 1: Devotion Emotion," which is available for download at http://store.northpoint.org/why-worry-part-one-devotion -emotion.html.

CHAPTER 6: WHEN YOU NOTICE GOD, THEN GOD WILL REVEAL HIS PRESENCE

1. If you're familiar with the TV series *24*, you know that Valencia was destroyed by a nuclear bomb in the fourth hour of season six. Before that, it was a beautiful suburban town.
2. It was a new construction, the numbers weren't up yet, and the contractor thought we meant lot 126; but we meant lot 122. Long story. But it was rather embarrassing when I tried to confront the people who'd moved into what we thought was our house.
3. John 14:8, NIV.
4. John 14:9, NIV.
5. Chris Rice. 2002. "Smell the Color 9." On *Smell the Color 9*. Rocketown Records.
6. Deuteronomy 14:21.
7. See Genesis 37:17-28; 50:15-21.
8. Genesis 12:1, author's paraphrase.
9. See Genesis 12:1-4.
10. See Exodus 2:11-15.
11. Colossians 1:15.
12. Romans 1:20.
13. Psalm 19:1-4, NIV.
14. Romans 1:21.
15. Romans 1:21-23.
16. Psalm 19:7-10.
17. See 1 Kings 19:1-13.

CHAPTER 7: WHEN YOU INVEST IN GOD'S KINGDOM, THEN GOD WILL INVEST IN YOURS

1. Matthew 20:21.
2. Matthew 20:22-23.
3. See Luke 9:23.
4. 2 Corinthians 9:6, NIV.
5. Mark 10:21, NIV.
6. Malachi 3:8-9, NIV.
7. Matthew 22:21.
8. Matthew 23:23, NIV.
9. See 1 Corinthians 16:1-2.
10. See 1 Timothy 6:17-19.
11. I am grateful for the teaching of Barry Cameron in this area.
12. Malachi 3:10, NIV.

13. Malachi 3:10-11, NIV.
14. See Philippians 4:10-13.

CHAPTER 8: WHEN YOU SHOW KINDNESS TO OTHERS, THEN GOD WILL SHOW THEM GRACE

1. 2 Corinthians 5:14, 17-20, NIV.
2. Luke 19:10.
3. Matthew 5:14-16, NIV.
4. Romans 2:4, NIV.
5. See Mark 2:1-5; Luke 5:17-19.
6. Mark 2:5.
7. See Mark 5:1-20.
8. Mark 5:19.
9. See Matthew 14:13-21; Mark 6:30-44; Luke 9:10-17; John 6:1-15.
10. 2 Corinthians 5:17.
11. John 9:25, NIV, italics added. I'm grateful to Bill Hybels for his teaching on this concept in the Just Walk across the Room sermon series.

CHAPTER 9: WHEN YOU PLACE YOUR HOPE IN GOD, THEN GOD WILL GIVE YOU HOPE

1. Romans 8:28.
2. Romans 5:5.

CHAPTER 10: THE WHEN/THEN PARTNERSHIP LIFE

1. See 1 Corinthians 11:20-34.
2. Philippians 4:13, NKJV.
3. Psalm 23:1, NKJV.
4. See Matthew 7:24-27.
5. Matthew 16:24.
6. 1 John 2:6, author's paraphrase.
7. 1 Corinthians 8:1, NIV.
8. Hafiz, *The Gift*, trans. Daniel Ladinsky (New York: Penguin, 1999).

acknowledgments

Lorrie. You continue to be the funniest person I know, the most beautiful woman I've ever seen, and my favorite person to be around. Your faithful dedication, support, and encouragement continue to be the greatest gifts to me outside of God's grace.

Lindsey and Sidney. Thank you for letting me tell stories about you . . . even though you make me pay you. And thank you for teaching me far more than I'll ever teach you. Your trust in your earthly father shows me how to respond to my heavenly Father.

Michael DeFazio. Thank you for helping make this book so much better than my idea on a napkin. Your wisdom and your contributions to this work are a blessing.

Fred Gray, Daryn Teague, Calvin Hedman, Sun Choi, Terry Meyer, Debbie Robert, Ryan Judd, Tim Hunten, Brennan Conklin, Stan Lubeck. Serving with you at RLC has made life and this book a light load, due to the many hands.

Mark Mears, Sean Costello, Danny Caudillo, Josh Heyer.

Your artistry and vision made this work and its promotion a reality.

Don Gates. This book would not have happened without you. Thanks for believing in me.

Jillian VandeWege, Sarah Atkinson, Sharon Leavitt, Jan Long Harris, Nancy Clausen, and all the people at Tyndale House Publishers. I can't thank you enough for taking a chance on me.

Dave Lindstedt. Every time I read your editing of my work, I thought, "Yeah! That's what I meant!" Thanks for saying it so much better than I could.

Caleb Kaltenbach. Thanks for making me do this. And thanks for every time when, while promoting your book, you mentioned mine. You are far too gracious to me.

Steve Meyers, Kevin Osborn, Mark Weigt, Monte Wilkinson, Mike Breaux. Your friendship and encouragement keep wind in my sails.

Dr. John Walker. Add me to the list of thousands you've influenced to stay in the game. Your investment in my life is nothing short of a blessing from God.

Shane Philip. I have no idea why you invested in such a goofy kid in high school, and why you continue to do so today. But I can honestly say that you have changed my life.

Bob, Mary, and April. Thank you for unconditional love and consistent forgiveness. And for giving me a home where Jesus was welcomed.

Jerry and Rose Miller. You two break the stereotype of in-laws. Thank you for welcoming me into your family and giving me the gift of your daughter.

The staff and people of Real Life Church. Thank you for letting me be your pastor. Your passion to help people find and follow Jesus keeps me getting out of bed in the morning.

Pete Wilson, Jud Wilhite, Larry Osborne, Sheila Walsh, Gene Appel, Ron Edmondson, and John Weece. Thank you so much for your encouragement and support. You have been mentors to me and have given me far more than I will ever be able to repay.

about the author

RUSTY GEORGE is the lead pastor of Real Life Church in Valencia, California. Born in Oklahoma, he spent his childhood in Wichita, Kansas, before attending Ozark Christian College in Joplin, Missouri, where he played basketball and earned bachelor's degrees in biblical studies and preaching. After graduation, he became the college pastor at Southland Christian Church in Lexington, Kentucky, where he had previously served two summers as an intern. In his nine years at Southland, Rusty moved to young-adult pastor and age-level director while also attending Cincinnati Christian Seminary.

After considering an opportunity to join some friends who were planting a church in North Carolina, Rusty got a call from his friend Kyle Idleman, who was the founder and lead pastor of Real Life Church. Kyle had been offered a position at another church, and he recommended Rusty as his successor at RLC. Though moving to California was certainly a change for Rusty and his wife, Lorrie, it quickly became home.

Since 2003, Rusty has led RLC through many changes, including the purchase of land, the construction of an eco-friendly building in the middle of town, and incredible growth from their original meetings in a 285-seat movie theater at the mall to a multicampus church where more than six thousand people now gather every weekend.

Rusty and Lorrie live in Valencia with their two daughters, Lindsey and Sidney.